THE
DEFICIT
DILEMMA

THE CHANGING DOMESTIC PRIORITIES SERIES

Listed below are the titles published to date in the Changing Domestic Priorities Series

THE REAGAN EXPERIMENT
An Examination of Economic and Social Policies under the Reagan Administration (1982), John L. Palmer and Isabel V. Sawhill, editors

HOUSING ASSISTANCE FOR OLDER AMERICANS
The Reagan Prescription (1982), James P. Zais, Raymond J. Struyk, and Thomas Thibodeau

MEDICAID IN THE REAGAN ERA
Federal Policy and State Choices (1982), Randall R. Bovbjerg and John Holahan

WAGE INFLATION
Prospects for Deceleration (1983), Wayne Vroman

OLDER AMERICANS IN THE REAGAN ERA
Impacts of Federal Policy Changes (1983), James R. Storey

FEDERAL HOUSING POLICY AT PRESIDENT REAGAN'S MID-TERM
(1983), Raymond J. Struyk, Neil Mayer, John Tuccillo

STATE AND LOCAL FISCAL RELATIONS IN THE EARLY 1980s
(1983), Steven D. Gold

THE DEFICIT DILEMMA
Budget Policy in the Reagan Era (1983), Gregory B. Mills and John L. Palmer

THE DEFICIT DILEMMA

BUDGET POLICY IN THE REAGAN ERA

Gregory B. Mills
John L. Palmer

The Changing Domestic Priorities Series
John L. Palmer and Isabel V. Sawhill, Editors

THE URBAN INSTITUTE PRESS · WASHINGTON, D.C.

Copyright © 1983
THE URBAN INSTITUTE
2100 M Street, N.W.
Washington, D.C. 20037

Library of Congress Cataloging in Publication Data

Mills, Gregory B., date
    The deficit dilemma.
    (The Changing domestic priorities series)
    Includes bibliographical references.
    1. Budget—United States. 2. Deficit financing—United States.
I. Palmer, John Logan. II. Title. III. Series.
HJ2051.M53   1983   353.0072'2   83-16886
ISBN 0-87766-327-0

Printed in the United States of America

THE URBAN INSTITUTE is a nonprofit policy research and educational organization established in Washington, D.C. in 1968. Its staff investigates the social and economic problems confronting the nation and government policies and programs designed to alleviate such problems. The Institute disseminates significant findings of its research through the publications program of its Press. The Institute has two goals for work in each of its research areas: to help shape thinking about societal problems and efforts to solve them, and to improve government decisions and performance by providing better information and analytic tools.

Through work that ranges from broad conceptual studies to administrative and technical assistance, Institute researchers contribute to the stock of knowledge available to public officials and to private individuals and groups concerned with formulating and implementing more efficient and effective government policy.

Conclusions or opinions expressed in Institute publications are those of the authors and do not necessarily reflect the views of other staff members, officers or trustees of the Institute, or of any organizations which provide financial support to the Institute.

Advisory Board of the
Changing Domestic Priorities Project

CONTENTS

FOREWORD xi

ACKNOWLEDGMENTS xiii

ABOUT THE AUTHORS xiv

1. INTRODUCTION AND SUMMARY 1

2. PRESIDENT REAGAN'S BUDGET OBJECTIVES 5

The President's Prescription for Revenues, Outlays, and the Deficit 5

The Administration's Tax Cuts As a Response to Rising Tax Burdens 8

The Defense Buildup As a Move to Restore the Nation's Military Capabilities 10

The Need for Nondefense Program Restraint 12

Reversing the Trend of Growing Deficits 13

Comparison of Administration Proposals with Alternative Baseline Projections 15

3. THE BUDGETARY CONSEQUENCES OF POLICY CHANGES UNDER PRESIDENT REAGAN 19

Broad Budget Outcomes 20

Changes in Revenues 23

Changes in Defense Outlays   26

Changes in Nondefense Program Spending   26

Competing Explanations for the Rise in Projected
    Deficits   27

4. HOW SERIOUS IS THE DEFICIT PROBLEM?   31

Structural Deficits   32

Why Are Deficits Undesirable?   34

What Projected Deficit Path Should Be Sought?   38

5. STRATEGIES TO REDUCE THE DEFICIT   41

Fiscal Year 1984 and Beyond: The President's Budget
    and the Congressional Budget Resolution   42

Opportunities and Prospects for Deficit Reduction   47

A Concluding Assessment   55

NOTES   59

TABLES

1 President Reagan's Original Budget Program   7
2 Government Revenues   8
3 Composition of Federal Revenues by Source   10
4 Federal Outlays for National Defense   11
5 Federal Outlays for Nondefense Programs   12
6 Federal Deficits and Net Interest Outlays   14
7 Projection of Federal Revenues, Outlays, and Deficits
       under Pre-Reagan Policies   16
8 Projection of Federal Policies as of September 1983   20
9 Sources of Increase in Projected Federal Deficits   22
10 Revenue Effects of ERTA and TEFRA   25
11 The Structural Component of Past and Projected
       Federal Deficits   33
12 Federal Deficits and Net Saving   36
13 Alternative Deficit Reduction Plans   44
14 Nondefense Program Outlays—Projected Growth and
       the President's Proposed Reductions   48
15 Increase in Federal Revenues under Selected Tax
       Measures   54

FOREWORD

This volume is part of the Changing Domestic Priorities project of The Urban Institute. The project is examining the shifts that are occurring in the nation's economic and social policies under the Reagan administration and analyzing the effect of the changes on people, places, and institutions.

Sweeping changes in the federal budget have been central to President Reagan's plans for economic recovery. As a candidate in 1980 and upon taking office in 1981, Ronald Reagan proposed to ease the burden of federal taxes and strengthen the nation's defense capabilities, while balancing the budget through curtailed growth in federal domestic programs. The president enjoyed remarkable success in his first year, as Congress enacted major tax cuts, accelerated the pace of defense spending, and made unprecedented reductions in domestic outlays. However, the economy failed to respond as predicted by the administration, and the domestic spending restraint proved insufficient to prevent enormous federal deficits. Through 1982 and into 1983, the president sought to preserve his tax and defense policies, while proposing to reduce the deficit largely through further cuts in domestic spending. Congress increasingly resisted the administration's proposals and moderated the defense buildup, rejected many of the president's requested nondefense cuts, and initiated tax increases well beyond the administration's proposals. The president and Congress now appear unable to reach consensus on further fiscal actions. This political impasse prevails while the deficit is projected to reach levels never before experienced in peacetime.

This book examines the political and economic predicament posed by large federal deficits. It describes how the federal budget outlook

xi

has evolved under President Reagan and assesses the need for future measures to reduce the deficit. The authors first describe President Reagan's original budget program in light of the budgetary trends he was seeking to reverse. The report explains how economic developments and newly enacted legislation both served to worsen the deficit outlook. Then the economic implications of large deficits and the strategies for narrowing the projected gap between federal revenues and outlays are addressed.

Large federal deficits normally occur during recessions and remain during the early stages of recovery. Such deficits are even welcome, as they serve to stimulate economic activity. Our current tax and spending policies, however, would yield large deficits even in a fully recovered economy. These policies thus endanger our long-term economic prospects, as heightened government borrowing weakens the chances for sustaining both strong growth and modest inflation.

In this book, the authors argue that politicians cannot afford to delay budgetary action in the false hope that stronger short-term economic performance will somehow ease the eventual clash between public and private borrowing demands. Inaction serves only to limit the available legislative options.

This study finds the disparity between projected federal revenues and outlays so great as to require action on all three major fronts for reducing the deficit: tax increases, a scaleback in the planned defense buildup, and further restraint on domestic spending. The policy decisions faced by the president and Congress are indeed difficult. Such decisions raise fundamental questions about the acceptable level of federal tax burdens, defense capabilities, and domestic program commitments.

The authors conclude that, given the pragmatic limits to spending control, as much as two-thirds or more of the desired deficit reduction may have to come through tax increases. Whether or not sufficient action is ultimately taken by the president and Congress, the need to reduce the federal deficit is an issue that will dominate the national policy debate for years to come.

John L. Palmer
Isabel V. Sawhill
Editors
Changing Domestic Priorities Series

ACKNOWLEDGMENTS

We wish to acknowledge our debt to those who enabled us to complete this study of a mounting U.S. public debt. Essential information was supplied by the staff of the Budget Analysis Division of the Congressional Budget Office, especially Paul Van de Water, Kathy Ruffing, and other members of the Projections Unit. Isabel Sawhill of The Urban Institute offered constructive suggestions on an earlier draft. Lisa Burns, Ann Guillot, and Mary Kate Smith skillfully prepared and edited the manuscript. Finally, we thank the Ford Foundation and the John D. and Katherine T. MacArthur Foundation for their financial support.

ABOUT THE AUTHORS

Gregory B. Mills is a research associate at The Urban Institute, where he is working on the Changing Domestic Priorities project. His prior research has focused upon federal policies to improve welfare administration, especially in the Aid to Families with Dependent Children Program. Before joining the Institute, Dr. Mills served as an economist in the Department of Health and Human Services. He is a contributing author of *The Reagan Experiment,* the Institute's recent examination of economic and social policies under the Reagan administration, and he also now serves as a consultant to the Food and Nutrition Service, Department of Agriculture.

John L. Palmer is codirector of The Urban Institute's Changing Domestic Priorities project. He has been an assistant professor of economics at Stanford University, a senior fellow in the Economic Studies Program of The Brookings Institution, an assistant secretary for the Department of Health and Human Services, and is now adjunct lecturer at the John F. Kennedy School of Government, Harvard University. Dr. Palmer is the author or editor of numerous articles and books including *The Reagan Experiment; Inflation, Unemployment and Poverty; Creating Jobs; Toward an Effective Income Support System*; and several chapters in the annual Brookings Institution's *Setting National Priorities* volumes.

CHAPTER 1

INTRODUCTION AND SUMMARY

President Reagan took office in 1981 with a pledge to reverse the major federal budgetary trends of the 1960s and 1970s. He proposed to cut taxes, accelerate the defense buildup, restrain domestic spending, and balance the federal budget; and the president was remarkably successful at enacting his initial proposals. Consequently, the federal tax burden has been lowered by more than 2 percent of gross national product (GNP), and defense expenditures have greatly increased their share of the federal budget at the expense of domestic spending. On the other hand, total federal spending has continued to rise as a percentage of GNP. We now face continuing annual deficits exceeding $200 billion, and neither the president nor Congress is proposing a workable plan to reduce these deficits, which threaten the long-term growth of the economy.

Why does the budget outlook diverge so dramatically from President Reagan's original plan? How serious a threat do the projected deficits pose to the economy? What strategies can Congress use to reduce the deficit? What are the prospects for legislative action? These concerns are and will remain, for the foreseeable future, dominant items on the public agenda.

The deficit presents a dilemma that is both economic and political. The economic quandary is the conflict between sustaining a recovery from the 1981-1982 recession and promoting the long-term prospects for the economy. The deficit reductions necessary to foster long-term growth will require tax increases and spending restraint that could stifle the current economic rebound. The political conflict bedeviling the administration and Congress lies in seeking to respond to public outcry over large deficits without inviting the re-

1

taliation of voters in specific populations and economic sectors that would be hardest hit by tax increases and spending cuts.

How did this predicament come about? President Reagan's principal objectives—lowered tax burdens, a bolstered national defense, and a balanced budget—could be attained simultaneously only if there were enormous restraint in federal domestic spending and an immediate, dramatic resurgence in economic growth. But the required spending restraint was not exercised. The unprecedented domestic spending cuts proposed by the administration and enacted by Congress in 1981 fell far short of what was necessary to prevent a rising deficit, for two reasons. First, Congress enacted more than the full measure of tax cuts and the defense buildup sought by the president in 1981. And, second, the most serious recession since the Great Depression intervened before strong economic growth began in 1983. As a result, the deficit, including off-budget spending, grew from $79 billion in fiscal year (FY) 1981 to $128 billion in FY 1982.

In response to this changed outlook, the president's FY 1983 budget request proposed even deeper domestic program cuts, while largely adhering to the enacted tax cuts and defense buildup and accepting a continuation of deficits at an unprecedented level. During 1982 Congress overwhelmingly rejected this scenario and instead passed a major tax increase, enacted modest additional domestic cuts, and scaled back slightly the continuation of the president's defense buildup. Nevertheless, the worsening economy put the deficit on a path exceeding $200 billion in 1983 and $300 billion by the decade's end. During 1983 the long-term deficit outlook under current policies has improved somewhat. An initially strong economic recovery from the recession and Social Security financing reforms have brought the projected deficit down below $300 billion for 1988. Unfortunately, little potential exists for continued reduction in future deficits owing to a stronger than expected recovery. These future deficits are predominantly structural—reflecting a fundamental imbalance between current taxing and spending policies that will persist even in a high-employment economy.

More importantly, such large projected deficits are simply not compatible with sustained, noninflationary economic growth. Although the recovery from the recession may be encouraged by the expansionary fiscal policy, the need for federal borrowing will soon strain the market for available credit. If these credit demands are not met through an accommodating monetary policy, interest rates will rise, discouraging business investment and the purchase of homes, autos, and other interest-sensitive consumer durables. High interest rates will maintain the dollar's strength in foreign currency markets, thus hurting American exports and helping foreign imports. While government spending would support a large public sector, the contribution of the private economy to national output would decline. Although the Federal Reserve could moderate this slowdown of economic activity by providing additional credit through its own purchase of government securities, the resulting monetary growth would likely rekindle inflation.

To avoid such a tradeoff between economic growth and inflation, the president and Congress must act to bring the deficit gradually down to a more reasonable level. An appropriate intermediate goal for the structural deficit would be about one percent of GNP, which is similar to the level experienced during the 1960s. This contrasts with currently projected levels of between 4 and 5 percent. To attain such a target over a five-year period would require tax increases and reductions in program spending that would amount annually to over $150 billion by FY 1988.

Measured against this target, neither the president's FY 1984 budget plan nor the congressional budget resolution for FY 1984 proposes sufficient action. The president's proposed deficit reductions are slightly more ambitious than those of Congress, but even they achieve only two-thirds of the desired long-term impact. If the prescribed deficit target is to be met, both the president and Congress must reconsider their positions on the three major fronts for deficit reduction: tax increases, reductions in the planned defense buildup, and domestic spending restraint. The defense restraint advocated by Congress would save $22 billion annually by 1988, while the reductions that the president requested in domestic programs amount to $52 billion annually by 1988. These amounts are probably the upper bounds for feasible action in each area. Together, however, they would achieve only one-half of the $150 billion target. Future annual revenue increases may thus need to exceed not only the $55 billion amount proposed by the president for 1988, most of which is conditional and temporary, but also the somewhat higher revenue gain implied by the congressional plan. In fact, the difficulties in achieving further outlay reductions throughout the budget suggest that permanent tax increases would have to effect as much as two-thirds of the prescribed deficit reduction.

To go further in outlining a deficit reduction plan would require more detailed policy judgments, with the following considerations in mind. To the extent that tax increases are to occur, the equity and efficiency of our present tax system are best enhanced by relying as much as possible on base-broadening measures rather than on tax rate increases. To the extent that defense outlays are to be restrained, our defense capabilities are best preserved through a scaleback of planned weapons purchases rather than through reducing current readiness. And to the extent that domestic spending growth is cut, those programs primarily responsible for fueling such growth—the so-called middle-class entitlement programs—will need to be scrutinized. In particular, any serious effort to reduce domestic spending without further restraining outlays in Social Security and Medicare would entail drastic reductions in other nondefense programs.

The prospects are dim for near-term legislative action that would yield the appropriate long-term deficit reduction. But if a concerted bipartisan effort is not mounted until 1985, options to avert undesirable economic consequences will shrink considerably. Obviously, only elected officials who place fiscal responsibility above partisan political advantage can best serve the national interest.

This book examines the changing federal budget under President Reagan—how developments up to September 1983 have affected the budget, and how the stage has been set for future budgetary choices. Chapter 2 considers President Reagan's initial budget plan against an historical backdrop. Chapter 3 discusses how congressional action on taxes and spending combined with changing economic conditions to alter the projected budget outlook that prevailed when President Reagan assumed office. Chapter 4 reviews the economic problems posed by large deficits. Finally, chapter 5 examines the deficit reduction plans put forward by the president and Congress in their FY 1984 budget proposals and addresses the policy tradeoffs that must be considered in reducing the deficit.

CHAPTER 2

PRESIDENT REAGAN'S BUDGET OBJECTIVES

The budget reforms that Ronald Reagan proposed as a presidential candidate in 1980 and as president in 1981 included a major reduction in tax burdens, rapid defense growth, and a balanced budget. These policies were a response to the widespread dissatisfaction with budgetary trends of the 1960s and 1970s—increasing federal tax burdens, no growth in inflation-adjusted defense spending, and rising federal deficits. The success of the president's plan depended critically upon considerable restraint in the growth of nondefense program spending and upon an immediate, strong, and sustained revival in economic growth.

This chapter first describes the key elements of the administration's original budget. It then discusses the historical context for the proposed tax cuts, defense buildup, nondefense spending restraint, and consequent deficit reduction. Finally, the president's program is contrasted with the budgetary outlook associated with no change in federal tax and spending policies.

The President's Prescription for Revenues, Outlays, and the Deficit

Within a month of taking office, President Reagan presented a four-part program to reduce inflation and promote economic growth. He announced the "Program for Economic Recovery" before a joint session of Congress on February 18, 1981. It included tax reductions, a slowdown in federal spending growth leading to a balanced budget, regulatory relief, and monetary restraint as necessary measures to

5

combat stagflation, the combination of a stagnating economy and rapid inflation. Monetary restraint was expected to curb inflation, and stronger and more sustained economic growth was to result from the tax cuts, deregulation, and spending restraint. The tax cuts were to play a central role, providing a supply side boost to the economy by promoting savings, investment, work effort, and productivity. The result was predicted to be annual real (inflation-adjusted) growth of GNP in excess of 4 percent during calendar years 1982-1986, with annual inflation declining to below 5 percent by 1986. (During the 1970-1980 period, real GNP had grown at an annual pace of 3 percent, with inflation steadily increasing to above 9 percent.) In essence the president embraced a set of tax and defense policies that could be reconciled with his balanced-budget objective only through extremely optimistic economic projections and large reductions in domestic spending.

The administration's tax and spending proposals were submitted to the Congress on March 10, 1981 as revisions to President Carter's budget proposals for FY 1982. The major provisions were as follows:

- a succession of three 10 percent reductions in personal income tax rates on July 1 of 1981, 1982, and 1983;
- accelerated depreciation provisions in the corporate income tax, shortening the depreciable lives of buildings, vehicles, and equipment;
- a five-year path of national defense outlay increases reflecting annual real growth of about 9 percent;
- a reduction in on- and off-budget nondefense program outlays of about $50 billion in 1982 and $100 billion annually by 1986, relative to baseline projections of pre-Reagan policies;[1] and
- additional unspecified spending reductions amounting annually to $30 billion in 1983 and more than $40 billion for 1984-1986, measured against baseline projections.

The budgetary shifts implied by these policies and the administration's economic forecast were truly enormous by historical standard. The expected economic recovery, along with the planned reductions in federal domestic spending, were to bring revenues into balance with total outlays by 1986, despite the large tax cuts and defense buildup (table 1). The administration indicated at the time

TABLE 1

PRESIDENT REAGAN'S ORIGINAL BUDGET PROGRAM
(FY 1982–FY 1986)

	FY 1981	FY 1982	FY 1983	FY 1984	FY 1985	FY 1986
	Percentage of GNP					
Revenues	21.1	20.4	19.7	19.3	19.3	19.5
Outlays (including off-budget)	23.9	22.3	20.6	19.5	19.4	19.1
National defense	5.7	5.9	6.3	6.4	6.9	7.1
Nondefense programs	15.9	14.3	12.5	11.4	11.0	10.6
Net interest	2.3	2.1	1.9	1.7	1.5	1.3
Total deficit (surplus)	2.8	1.9	0.9	0.2	0.0	(0.4)
	Billions of Constant (FY 1972) Dollars					
Outlays National Defense	77.8	83.0	92.6	98.4	110.8	118.9
Nondefense programs	213.9	197.0	180.1	172.6	173.6	176.6

SOURCE: Office of Management and Budget, "Federal Government Finances," March 1981, pp. 6, 12, 72, 77, and 84.

NOTE: Based upon the Reagan administration's economic forecast and technical assumptions. The unspecified outlay reductions included by the administration in the estimates for FY 1983–FY 1986 are assumed to come entirely from nondefense programs.

that even further tax reductions would be sought, in line with the projected continued decline in outlays as a percentage of GNP.

In the presence of a rising GNP share devoted to national defense, the drop in total outlays relative to GNP implied a massive reversal in the federal domestic commitment embodied in the policies President Reagan inherited. Adjusted for inflation, nondefense outlays were to fall at an annual rate of more than 4 percent between 1981 and 1986, after having risen at an annual pace exceeding 6 percent during the previous twenty years. The president's projections for defense outlays, nondefense program spending, and interest outlays on the public debt for 1986 resembled the pattern of budget shares prevailing in 1971. This reversal in historical trends was embodied not only in the administration's original proposals, but also in its FY 1983 budget, submitted to the Congress in February 1982.

The Administration's Tax Cuts As a Response to Rising Tax Burdens

The federal tax burden increased substantially between 1961 and 1981, most dramatically in the last five years of the period. In contrast, state and local tax burdens rose through the mid-1970s, but declined thereafter. The result was a steadily rising total tax burden since the late 1960s, with tax burdens for both federal and total revenues reaching peacetime highs in 1981 (table 2).

The growth in federal receipts during the 1976-1981 period was primarily because of inflation and the accompanying process known as bracket creep. During inflationary periods, personal and corporate incomes must rise simply to keep pace with price increases. However, these inflation-induced additions to income are taxed at progressively higher rates. Furthermore, the real value of those exemptions, deductions, and credits that are fixed in dollar terms is eroded through price increases. As a result, taxes come to represent a higher fraction of income, even though before-tax purchasing power is unchanged. Nearly three-fourths of the rise in federal revenues during the 1976-1981 period could be attributed to these effects, as inflation proceeded at an annual rate in excess of 8 percent during the five-year period.[2]

National economic growth during the 1976-1981 period also contributed to the rise in the federal tax burden. After adjusting for inflation, GNP increased at an average annual rate of 3 percent

TABLE 2

GOVERNMENT REVENUES
(FY 1961–FY 1981)

	FY 1961– FY 1965	FY 1966– FY 1970	FY 1971– FY 1975	FY 1976– FY 1980	FY 1981
	Percentage of GNP				
Federal	18.2	19.2	18.6	19.2	20.8
State and local	8.4	9.2	10.6	10.4	9.7
Total	26.6	28.4	29.2	29.6	30.5

SOURCE: Office of Management and Budget, "Total Government Finances," February 1983, p. 2; and Department of Commerce, "U.S. National Income and Product Accounts: Revised Estimates," *Survey of Current Business*, July 1983.

NOTE: The multiyear entries are computed as the average of the corresponding five fiscal years.

between 1976 and 1981, despite one brief recession in early 1980 and the onset of another in late 1981. Because of the progressivity of tax rates, such real growth caused revenues to rise proportionately more than national income, thus pushing upward the ratio of tax receipts to GNP.

Changes in tax policies were also partly responsible for rising tax burdens. Congress did liberalize personal exemptions, deductions, and credits in the individual income tax system through legislation in 1976, 1977, and 1978; Congress also lowered the statutory tax rates for both individual and corporate income taxes in 1978. These provisions, however, were more than offset by a series of legislative changes that tended to raise federal taxes. Chief among these were the increases in Social Security payroll taxes enacted in 1977 to stave off the impending insolvency of the system[3] and the enactment in 1979 of the windfall profits tax on income from domestically produced oil.

The 1960s and 1970s saw a large rise in both average and marginal federal tax rates for the typical taxpayer. Consider a husband-wife family with two children, with family income at the national median comprised entirely of the husband's earnings.[4] Between 1960 and 1980, this family's federal income tax and Social Security payroll tax (employee share only) increased as a percentage of income from 10.1 to 17.5 percent.[5] The family's federal marginal tax rate, the rate at which an additional dollar of income was taxed, increased from 20 to 30 percent.[6]

The rise in average federal tax rates during the 1960s and 1970s was more pronounced for lower-income taxpayers than for the well-to-do. Consider once again a four-person family, but with income at one-half the median income.[7] This family's federal income tax and Social Security payroll tax more than doubled as a percentage of income from 1960 to 1980, from 5.8 to 12.1 percent, whereas the average tax rate of the family at twice the national median increased less than two-thirds, from 13.2 to 21.5 percent.[8]

The composition of federal revenues by tax source and the distribution of the tax burden by income class were both altered significantly by these economic and policy developments (table 3). Because the individual income tax is more sensitive than the corporate income tax to inflation-induced income increases, the rapid inflation of 1976-1981 served to raise the proportion of federal revenues obtained through individual income taxation. The share of corporate taxes declined during the same interval, following an even more dramatic earlier drop between 1966 and 1971 because of corporate

TABLE 3

COMPOSITION OF FEDERAL REVENUES BY SOURCE
(FY 1961–FY 1981)

	FY 1961	FY 1966	FY 1971	FY 1976	FY 1981
	Percentage of Total Federal Revenues				
Individual income taxes	43.8	42.4	46.1	44.2	47.7
Corporate income taxes	22.2	23.0	14.3	13.9	10.2
Social insurance taxes and contributions	17.4	19.5	25.3	30.5	30.5
All other taxes[a]	16.6	15.1	14.3	11.4	11.6
Total	100.0	100.0	100.0	100.0	100.0

NOTE: Office of Management and Budget, "Federal Government Finances," February 1983, pp. 10–11.

a.   Includes excise taxes, estate and gift taxes, customs duties, and miscellaneous receipts.

rate reductions, liberalized investment tax credits, and more generous depreciation provisions. Social insurance taxes and contributions—primarily the payroll taxes for Social Security, Medicare, and unemployment insurance—were the fastest rising source of federal revenues. Their share grew rapidly during 1961-1976 and then remained constant during the 1976-1981 period of rapid growth in the federal revenue total.

The Defense Buildup As a Move to Restore the Nation's Military Capabilities

The twenty-year period preceding the Reagan administration began and ended with defense outlays at virtually the same dollar level, after adjusting for inflation.[9] This translated into a decline in the GNP share of defense outlays by more than one-third (table 4). Accompanying this overall trend was a shift in the composition of defense spending. An increasing share of national defense outlays went for current operating expenses in defense-related activities, primarily the payroll for active personnel and the operation and maintenance cost of existing military facilities and equipment. Meanwhile, the costs of retirement benefits for former military personnel more than quadrupled as a percentage of the defense budget. This meant that the share of outlays for military investment—weapons procurement, research and development, and construction—declined from more than 45 percent to less than 35 percent of defense

TABLE 4

FEDERAL OUTLAYS FOR NATIONAL DEFENSE
(FY 1961–FY 1981)

	FY 1961	FY 1966	FY 1971	FY 1976	FY 1981
	Billions of Dollars				
Constant (FY 1972) dollars	74.6	76.3	81.4	67.1	76.4
	Percentage of GNP				
Current dollars	9.2	7.6	7.3	5.5	5.5
	Percentage of Total National Defense Outlays[a]				
By category					
Military operating expenses[b]	48.1	54.2	57.3	59.0	54.9
Military retirement benefits	1.8	2.9	4.5	8.2	8.6
Military investment[c]	45.6	41.5	36.5	31.1	34.2
All other[d]	4.5	1.4	1.8	1.7	2.3
Total	100.0	100.0	100.0	100.0	100.0

SOURCE: Office of Management and Budget, "Federal Government Finances," February 1983, pp. 24–26, 81–83, and 88–90; and Department of Commerce, "National Income and Product Accounts: Revised Estimates," *Survey of Current Business*, July 1983.

a. Percentage distribution for FY 1961 was unavailable. Data shown are for FY 1962.

b. Includes expenses for military personnel and military operations and maintenance, minus deductions for associated offsetting receipts.

c. Includes expenses for military procurement, research and development, and construction.

d. Includes expenses for atomic energy and other nonmilitary defense-related activities, minus deductions for associated offsetting receipts.

spending. Concern over the underfunding of defense was principally addressed at this declining emphasis on the development of future military capabilities.

The downward trend in real defense spending was reversed during the late 1970s. In establishing U.S. commitments to the NATO alliance, President Carter pledged the country to 3 percent real defense growth, a trend that was achieved from 1979 to 1981. In fact, the FY 1981 budget authority enacted by Congress for Defense Department military activities represented a 12 percent real increase over the prior year; the investment component experienced a 22 percent real increase.[10]

The Need for Nondefense Program Restraint

In marked contrast to national defense outlays, inflation-adjusted spending on nondefense programs more than tripled between 1961 and 1981 (table 5). This reflected an annual real increase exceeding 6 percent from 1961 to 1981.[11] Although substantial growth occurred during this period in all three major components of nondefense program spending—payments for individuals, other grants to state and local governments, and other direct federal operations—the rapid growth in benefit payments to individuals was clearly dominant. Annual real growth in benefit payments averaged nearly 8 percent between 1961 and 1981. Outlays for benefit programs

TABLE 5

FEDERAL OUTLAYS FOR NONDEFENSE PROGRAMS
(FY 1961–FY 1981)

	FY 1961	FY 1966	FY 1971	FY 1976	FY 1981
	Billions of Constant (FY 1972) Dollars				
Payment for individuals	37.2	45.5	81.8	134.9	162.9
Other grants to state and local governments	6.8	12.2	18.2	27.4	25.6
Other direct federal operations	21.6	36.9	25.7	30.0	37.6
Total	65.6	94.6	125.7	192.3	226.1
	Percentage of GNP				
Payments for individuals	5.4	5.0	7.6	10.8	11.0
Other grants to state and local governments	0.8	1.2	1.7	2.3	1.9
Other direct federal operations	2.5	3.6	2.3	2.5	2.7
Total	8.7	9.8	11.6	15.6	15.6
Addendum					
Total grants to state and local governments[a]					
Billions of constant (FY 1972) dollars	10.8	17.9	29.6	43.5	46.1
Percentage of GNP	1.4	1.8	2.7	3.6	3.3

SOURCE: Office of Management and Budget, "Federal Government Finances," February 1983, p. 81–92. Includes off-budget outlays.

a. Includes the portion of "payments for individuals" that is administered through state and local governments (such as Medicaid and Aid to Families with Dependent Children), in addition to "other grants to state and local governments."

targeted on the low-income population grew faster than this average, and spending on social insurance and other non-means-tested benefit programs grew less rapidly.

Several interrelated factors promoted the rapid increase in real benefit payments through the early 1970s. New programs, such as Medicaid, Medicare, and Food Stamps were introduced; the eligibility and benefit provisions of existing programs, such as Social Security and Aid to Families with Dependent Children (AFDC), were liberalized; economic and demographic shifts, such as the rapid growth in the aged and single-parent families, led to larger numbers of eligible persons; the participation rate rose among the eligible population as the Civil Rights movement and War on Poverty increased public awareness of the benefits to which persons were entitled and reduced the stigma attached to receiving them; and more generous federal funding provisions were adopted under joint federal-state financing arrangements. Although these sources of real growth exerted little influence by the late 1970s, inflation continued to drive nominal benefit outlays upward at an annual pace of nearly 12 percent during the 1976-1981 period.[12]

These various circumstances caused benefit payments to more than double as a percentage of GNP between 1961 and 1981, with virtually all of this increase coming by the mid-1970s. Other grants to state and local governments also more than doubled in their GNP share between 1961 and 1981. However, such grant outlays were declining by the end of this period, both as a percentage of GNP and in inflation-adjusted dollars after having peaked in 1978. Other direct federal operations grew as a percentage of GNP between 1961 and 1966, declined in the following decade, and then stabilized between 2.5 and 3.0 percent of GNP in the late 1970s.

Reversing the Trend of Growing Deficits

The budget developments of the 1960s and 1970s led to an increasing disparity between the revenue yield of federal tax policies and the financing requirements of federal program activities. The growth in tax burdens was surpassed by the growth in total outlays, and annual federal deficits crept upward both in dollars and as a percentage of GNP (table 6). In part this reflected the weakness of the economy. Higher levels of unemployment not only restrained the level of revenues, by curbing the growth of taxable incomes, but

TABLE 6

FEDERAL DEFICITS AND NET INTEREST OUTLAYS
(FY 1961–FY 1981)

	Total Deficit[a]		Net Interest Outlays[b]	
	Billions of Dollars	Percentage of GNP	Billions of Dollars	Percentage of GNP
Five-year averages				
1961–1965	—	0.8	—	1.3
1966–1970	—	0.9	—	1.4
1971–1975	—	1.9	—	1.5
1976–1980	—	3.0	—	1.7
Annual data				
1961	3.4	0.7	6.7	1.3
1966	3.8	0.5	9.4	1.3
1971	23.0	2.2	14.8	1.4
1976	73.7	4.5	26.7	1.6
1977	53.6	2.9	29.9	1.6
1978	59.2	2.8	35.4	1.7
1979	40.2	1.7	42.6	1.8
1980	73.8	2.9	52.5	2.0
1981	78.9	2.7	68.7	2.4

SOURCE: Office of Management and Budget, "Federal Government Finances," February 1983, pp. 5, 7, 70–71, and 88–90.

a. Includes off-budget outlays.

b. Interest payments on federal debt held by the public (including the Federal Reserve System) and interest paid on tax refunds, minus interest collected from federal agencies and the public.

also promoted a rise in outlays, through greater demands for unemployment insurance and means-tested entitlements such as Food Stamps, AFDC, and Medicaid. Even when adjusted for changes in the unemployment rate, however, federal deficits exhibited a clearly upward trend as a percentage of GNP.

Inflation served to moderate the growth of the more recent deficits, as bracket creep tended to spur revenue growth faster than the outlay growth associated with the automatic indexing of income transfers and discretionary inflation adjustments in other programs. However, the higher interest rates that accompanied inflation led to a dramatic rise in the level of interest payments necessary to finance the accumulating federal debt. The credit markets exacted a heavy price each time the government sought either to refinance its existing debt, as outstanding securities matured, or to service the newly created debt caused by current deficits. Annual net interest outlays nearly doubled as a percentage of GNP between 1961 and 1981.

Comparison of Administration Proposals with Alternative Baseline Projections

President Reagan's original budget proposals should be viewed not only in the context of evolving budget conditions during the 1960s and 1970s, but also in relation to the budget picture that might have resulted under a continuation of the policies he inherited (table 7). The latter perspective is relevant because economic and demographic changes would have altered budget outcomes from their 1981 pattern under any set of tax and spending policies.

What would have happened to tax burdens if there had been no changes in the tax law after President Reagan assumed office in 1981, and if the economy performed as forecast by the Reagan administration in early 1981?[13] If one assumes that the provisions of the individual income tax would have been adjusted to offset the bracket creep occurring from October 1981 onward, federal revenues would have grown from 21.4 percent of GNP in 1981 to 21.8 percent by 1986.[14] Even with the assumed adjustment for inflation, individual income taxes would have risen between 1981 and 1986 as a percentage of total federal revenues (from 47 to 49 percent) and as a percentage of taxable personal income (from 14 to 16 percent).

Defense spending had increased during 1979-1981 at an annual inflation-adjusted rate of 3 to 5 percent. Continued real outlay growth was inevitable in 1982, given the dramatic increase in budget authority for national defense that Congress had enacted the prior year and President Carter's support for 5 percent real growth in 1982.[15] The baseline assumption adopted here is that real spending would have grown 5 percent in 1982, 4 percent in 1983, and 3 percent from 1984 through 1986. The trend rate of growth for 1982-1986 would thus have been 3.6 percent, in excess of the NATO guideline announced by President Carter. Such annual increases would have led defense outlays to fall as a percentage of GNP from 5.6 percent in 1981 to 5.3 percent in 1986.

As noted earlier, the major sources of real growth in nondefense program spending had subsided by the time President Reagan took office. Without new legislative initiatives and with real growth sufficient only to maintain the unemployment rate at its 1981 level of

TABLE 7

PROJECTION OF FEDERAL REVENUES, OUTLAYS, AND DEFICITS
UNDER PRE-REAGAN POLICIES
(FY 1981–FY 1986)

	FY 1981	FY 1982	FY 1983	FY 1984	FY 1985	FY 1986
	Percentage of GNP					
Revenues	21.4	21.5	21.5	21.5	21.6	21.8
Outlays (including off-budget)	23.9	23.5	22.3	21.2	20.5	20.0
National defense	5.6	5.6	5.5	5.4	5.3	5.3
Nondefense programs	16.0	15.6	14.8	14.1	13.8	13.5
Net interest	2.3	2.3	2.0	1.7	1.4	1.2
Total deficit (surplus)	2.5	2.0	0.8	(0.3)	(1.1)	(1.9)
	Billions of Dollars					
Addendum Total deficit (surplus)	71	64	28	(11)	(50)	(90)

SOURCE: Congressional Budget Office, *Baseline Budget Projections for Fiscal Years 1982–1986* (Washington, D.C.: GPO, 1981); unpublished data from the Congressional Budget Office; and authors' calculations.

NOTE: Estimated under the baseline economic forecast published in the above report. Projected revenues assume legislative action to offset bracket creep in the individual income tax; projected national defense outlays assume annual real growth of 5 percent in 1982, 4 percent in 1983, and 3 percent in 1984–1986; and projected nondefense program outlays assume full adjustment for inflation (and thus the maintenance of real service levels in all programs).

7.6 percent, such spending would have declined as a percentage of GNP by 1986. Health care financing programs would have risen faster than GNP as a result of continued health cost inflation at a rate exceeding that of general price increases. Their rapid growth, however, would have been more than offset by favorable demographic trends slowing the growth of all other programs, even assuming benefit levels to be fully adjusted for inflation. The administration's projected path of economic growth and unemployment—with the unemployment rate declining to 5.6 percent in 1986—would have moderated even further the growth in spending for means-tested transfers. The result of these forces was a projected GNP share for nondefense programs that was 13.5 percent in 1986, well below its expected 1981 level of 16.0 percent.

What would have happened to the federal deficit under a continuation of pre-Reagan policies with inflation adjustment of the personal income tax? With revenues rising modestly as a percentage of GNP, but with both defense and nondefense programs falling in their GNP shares, the deficit would have been eliminated by 1984 under the administration's economic forecast. Sizable federal surpluses would have occurred thereafter, approaching 2 percent of GNP by 1986.

When measured against this baseline projection of pre-Reagan policies, the Reagan administration's budget reforms constituted a substantial shift in the pattern of federal taxes and spending. By 1986 the large surplus projected under former policies was to be reduced in size through tax reductions exceeding the amount of expected spending cuts. The reductions in total spending were to occur through cuts in nondefense program outlays exceeding the increase in defense spending. This projected shift in the composition of federal program outlays toward national defense was dramatic. Whereas defense claimed less than 30 percent of noninterest outlays in 1981, and would have continued to do so through 1986 under a continuation of pre-Reagan policies, the administration's proposals would have increased the defense share to more than 40 percent.

As stated earlier, this reorientation in spending priorities—in the context of a decline in total federal spending as a percentage of GNP—implied huge cuts in domestic programs. Only some of these cuts were explicitly identified in the president's original proposals. The administration pinned its hopes for such spending restraint not only on its ability to reduce "fraud, abuse, and waste" but also on the spending discipline that presumably would be instilled in Congress through tax cuts and the need to reduce spending to avoid large deficits. Only with such presumed cuts in domestic programs and a forecast of very strong economic performance, could the administration assert that large tax cuts, a defense buildup, and a balanced budget could be achieved simultaneously.

CHAPTER 3

THE BUDGETARY CONSEQUENCES OF POLICY CHANGES UNDER PRESIDENT REAGAN

The Reagan administration enjoyed considerable early success in gaining congressional passage of its budget proposals. However, the economy failed to respond to the policies as the administration predicted. Instead of an economic recovery that was to enable a balanced budget by 1984, the country entered a prolonged recession in July 1981. Although the Congress enacted unprecedented spending reductions in nondefense programs, the budget outlook shifted toward enormous future deficits. The worsening state of the economy, in combination with tax cuts and increased defense outlays, resulted in a federal deficit that reached $128 billion in 1982 and that is projected under current policies to exceed $200 billion in 1983 and $250 billion by 1988.[1] The administration has attributed the deficit dilemma largely to unrestrained growth in entitlement programs, while others place the responsibility on the tax cuts and defense buildup.

This chapter reviews the recent changes in federal tax and spending policies and their implications for projected deficits. The shifts in projected levels of revenues, outlays, and the deficit are first examined, with attention to the respective importance of changes in policy and changes in the economy. This is followed by a description of the policy changes enacted in the separate areas of taxes, defense spending, and nondefense spending. The chapter ends with a discussion of competing explanations for the worsening budgetary outlook.

Broad Budget Outcomes

During the past two years, the federal budget has departed dramatically from the broad outcomes sought by the Reagan administration. Largely because of the economy's failure to respond as the administration predicted, federal revenues and outlays moved onto increasingly divergent paths. Although the president's policies were originally forecast by the administration to yield a surplus of 0.4 percent of GNP in 1986, current policies (including continuation of the president's requested defense buildup) and projected economic conditions imply a 1986 deficit of $236 billion, or 5.6 percent of GNP (table 8). This projected increase in the deficit as a percentage of GNP from 2.7 percent in 1981 can be attributed to a reduction in the federal tax burden by 2.1 percentage points of GNP and a rise

TABLE 8

PROJECTION OF FEDERAL POLICIES AS OF SEPTEMBER 1983
(FY 1983–FY 1988)

	Actual		Projected[a]			
	FY 1981	FY 1982	FY 1983	FY 1984	FY 1986	FY 1988
	Percentage of GNP					
Revenues	20.8	20.2	18.7	18.7	18.7	18.7
Outlays (including off-budget)	23.5	24.4	25.7	24.7	24.4	24.5
National defense	5.5	6.1	6.6	6.9	7.7	8.1
Nondefense programs	15.6	15.5	16.3	15.1	13.9	13.7
Net interest	2.4	2.8	2.7	2.7	2.7	2.7
Total deficit	2.7	4.2	7.0	6.0	5.6	5.8
	Billions of Dollars					
Addendum Total deficit	79	128	225	213	236	280

SOURCES: Congressional Budget Office, *Baseline Budget Projections for Fiscal Years 1984–1988* (Washington, D.C.: GPO, 1983); *The Economic and Budget Outlook: An Update* (Washington, D.C.: GPO, 1983); unpublished CBO tabulations; and authors' calculations.

a.   Estimated under the economic forecast adopted by Congress in passing its *First Concurrent Resolution on the Budget for Fiscal Year 1984.* Assumes adoption of the administration's defense request for FY 1984 and subsequent years, plus the continuation of all tax and spending policies enacted through August 1983 (including the emergency jobs legislation, Social Security amendments, and repeal of tax withholding on interest and dividend income).

in the outlay share of GNP by 0.9 percentage point. The projected fall in tax burdens exceeds that originally proposed by the administration, despite the tax increase of 1982 that offset one-third of the tax cut enacted in 1981. The projected outlay growth stands in marked contrast to the spending restraint embodied in the president's original program, whereby outlays were to fall as a percentage of GNP. By 1988 current policies will drive the deficit upward even further to an estimated $280 billion, or 5.8 percent of projected GNP.

To what extent has the budgetary outlook been worsened by the weakened economy? This question can be addressed by comparing present deficit projections with the pre-Reagan baseline discussed at the end of chapter 2. Each projection was based upon a separate set of assumptions regarding federal policies, economic performance, and the technical relationships that link budgetary outcomes with the prevailing policy and economic conditions. One can thus attribute the differences between the two projections to differences in these three sets of assumptions. On the basis of such a comparison for 1986, almost two-thirds of the shift toward larger deficits is because of the poorer-than-anticipated economic performance (table 9). Virtually all of the upward pressure on deficits posed by the disappointing performance of the economy was felt on the revenue side. The combination of lower economic growth and more moderate inflation (than originally projected by the administration) translates into a lower path of nominal GNP, leading to less taxable income and thus lower revenues. By 1986 this shift in expected economic conditions implies an annual revenue loss of $220 billion.

Further aggravating the long-term deficit outlook have been the changes in policy enacted thus far under President Reagan. Measured against the continuation of pre-Reagan policies as described in chapter 2, the changes in policy contribute $100 billion to annual deficits by 1986. This results primarily from lower revenues relative to the pre-Reagan baseline path. In addition, however, the policy changes will by 1986 increase outlays above the baseline levels projected under pre-Reagan policies. Contrary to the president's intentions, the drop in nondefense program outlays resulting from policy action is eventually exceeded by the increase in defense spending. Furthermore, higher interest outlays result from the increase in cumulative deficits owing to the tax cuts and net changes in program spending.

There thus seems to be no meaningful sense in which one could argue that the policies adopted under President Reagan have served

TABLE 9
SOURCES OF INCREASE IN PROJECTED FEDERAL DEFICITS
(FY 1982–FY 1986)

	FY 1982	FY 1983	FY 1984	FY 1985	FY 1986
Projected total deficit (surplus)			*Billions of Dollars*		
As of January 1981[a]	64	28	(11)	(50)	(90)
As of September 1983[b]	128	225	213	218	236
Increase in deficit	64	197	224	268	326
Sources of increase in deficit					
Changes in technical assumptions	−2	29	26	19	11
Changes in economic outlook	71	146	159	180	215
Revenues	49	131	157	179	220
Outlays	22	15	2	1	−5
Changes in policy	−5	22	39	69	100
Revenues	30	50	59	69	83
Outlays (see Addendum)	−35	−28	−20	0	17
Addendum					
Changes in policy—outlays	−35	−28	−20	0	17
Defense	3	13	30	51	69
Nondefense programs	−38	−41	−53	−58	−65
Net interest	0	0	3	7	13

SOURCES: Congressional Budget Office, *Baseline Budget Projections for Fiscal Years 1984–1988* (Washington, D.C.: GPO, 1983), pp. 18, 35, and 57; CBO estimates of legislation enacted in 1983 and net interest outlays as affected by shifts in revenues or program outlays; and authors' calculations.

a. Estimated under the baseline economic forecast published in Congressional Budget Office, *Baseline Budget Projections: Fiscal Years 1982–1986* (Washington, D.C.: GPO, 1981). Assumes annual real growth in defense outlays of 5 percent in 1982, 4 percent in 1983, and 3 percent in 1984–1986; also assumes no change in corporate tax provisions and nondefense program policies as of January 1981, with full adjustment for inflation in nondefense programs, and tax reductions to offset bracket creep in the individual income tax.

b. Estimated under the economic forecast adopted by Congress in passing its *First Concurrent Resolution on the Budget for Fiscal Year 1984*. Assumes adoption of the administration's defense request for FY 1984 and subsequent years, plus the continuation of all tax and spending policies enacted through August 1983 (including the emergency jobs legislation, Social Security amendments, and repeal of tax withholding on interest and dividend income).

to lower the overall rate of growth of federal outlays. To the extent that neither spending growth nor the deficit has been restrained, the administration's broadest budget objectives have not been met. On more specific budget objectives, however, the president has achieved considerable success. Tax burdens have certainly been reduced, defense outlays increased, and nondefense program spending cut in substantial amounts from the levels that would otherwise have been attained. Indeed, the administration's success on taxes and defense heightened the need for nondefense spending restraint even beyond what the president originally proposed, especially in the absence of the predicted immediate resurgence of the economy. As the administration failed to achieve the necessary restraint on nondefense spending and basically held to its tax and defense policies, budget projections came to show a pattern of extremely large and growing deficits.

Changes in Revenues

To the extent that the deteriorating budget outlook for the 1980s can be attributed to legislation enacted thus far under President Reagan, it is the policy changes on the revenue side that are responsible. The 1986 revenue loss associated with the recent tax changes is estimated under present economic assumptions to be $83 billion, as measured against the revenue yield anticipated under prior corporate tax laws and an indexed individual income tax. Along with an associated $23 billion rise in 1986 interest outlays because of higher debt financing requirements, the tax changes increase the 1986 deficit by $106 billion, or 2.5 percent of projected GNP. This shift was largely the net result of a landmark piece of tax-cutting legislation, the Economic Recovery Tax Act of 1981 (ERTA), and a major revenue-raising measure enacted the following year, the Tax Equity and Fiscal Responsibility Act of 1982 (TEFRA). In addition, an increase in the gasoline excise tax was enacted in the Highway Revenue Act of 1982, and higher revenues will result from the 1983 Social Security reforms.

The major provisions of ERTA were as follows: three successive reductions in 1981, 1982, and 1983 in individual income tax rates amounting to a cumulative, across-the-board reduction of 23 percent; a reduction in the "marriage penalty" by allowing two-earner couples to deduct a portion of the earned income of the lesser-earning spouse; the "indexing," starting in 1985, of tax brackets, the zero bracket amount, and the personal exemption in the individual income tax, to prevent the effective tax increases that occur as a result of bracket creep; and accelerated depreciation rules, allowing a faster write-off of capital expenditures.

The major tax provisons of TEFRA were a tightening of the investment tax credit, a partial repeal of the accelerated depreciation schedules and safe harbor leasing rules contained in ERTA;[2] tax withholding on interest and dividend income;[3] and further strengthened enforcement of existing tax rules. Starting in 1984, TEFRA will offset more than one-half of the annual corporate tax reduction granted through ERTA and about one-third of the total annual revenue loss due to ERTA (table 10). By 1986 more than one-half of the revenue gain associated with TEFRA will come from corporate income tax increases.

TEFRA was a remarkable legislative achievement—a major tax increase passed in the midst of midterm congressional elections. It had become all too apparent, even by the fall of 1981, that the weakness of the economy and the revenue loss associated with ERTA would create intolerably large future deficits. TEFRA was an attempt, spearheaded by the Republican leadership of the Senate and only belatedly and reluctantly supported by the president, to shore up the federal tax yield. However, TEFRA offset only a fraction of the revenue loss associated with the recession.

Estimates of the combined revenue impact of recent tax changes indicate an enormous shift in the level and composition of federal revenues. For 1988 the projected revenue yield of current tax policies will be 9 percent below that associated with a continuation of the pre-ERTA law, holding economic conditions constant. For the major revenue categories, the proportional impact in 1988 ranges from an 18 percent drop in individual income tax revenues to a 15 percent rise in excise taxes. (The latter change reflects primarily the 5-cent-a-gallon increase in the gasoline tax effective April 1, 1983.) The individual income tax is now projected to represent 45 percent of 1988 federal revenues, versus the 50 percent by 1988 as estimated under pre-ERTA law assuming inflation adjustments. Social insurance taxes will comprise 38 percent of 1988 receipts, compared to 33 percent in the pre-ERTA baseline projection.

One consequence of this shift in importance of the different revenue sources is that the projected tax structure is less progressive than it would otherwise have been. The more progressive forms of

TABLE 10

REVENUE EFFECTS OF ERTA AND TEFRA
(FY 1982–FY 1988)

	FY 1982	FY 1983	FY 1984	FY 1986	FY 1988	Cumulative, FY 1982– FY 1988
	Billions of dollars					
Individual income taxes						
ERTA[a]	−21	−50	−74	−91	−112	−529
TEFRA	0	5	10	13	18	72
Corporate income taxes						
ERTA	−9	−17	−26	−42	−43	−216
TEFRA	0	7	16	26	31	131
Other taxes						
ERTA	−1	−2	−4	−7	−11	−41
TEFRA	0	6	9	6	5	41
Total						
ERTA	−30	−70	−104	−141	−166	−787
TEFRA	0	18	35	45	54	244
	TEFRA Effect as a Percentage of ERTA Effect					
Individual income taxes	0	−10	−14	−14	−16	−14
Corporate income taxes	0	−41	−62	−62	−72	−61
Total	0	−26	−34	−32	−33	−31

SOURCES: Congressional Budget Office, *Baseline Budget Projections for Fiscal Years 1984–1988* (Washington, D.C.: GPO, 1983), pp. 27–28; and *Reducing the Deficit: Spending and Revenue Options* (Washington, D.C.: GPO, 1983), p. 238.

NOTE: ERTA is the Economic Recovery Tax Act of 1981; TEFRA is the Tax Equity and Fiscal Responsibility Act of 1982. The impact of TEFRA has been adjusted to reflect the subsequent repeal of the withholding requirement on interest and dividend income.

a. The individual income tax cut in ERTA is measured against a baseline projection that assumes indexing of individual tax provisions to offset bracket creep since October 1981.

taxation such as individual and corporate income taxes, whose burdens rise at higher income levels, are becoming less significant sources of revenue. Conversely, the government will be relying more upon more regressive taxes, such as social insurance and excise taxes.

Changes in Defense Outlays

Congress accepted the president's proposed defense buildup without revision during 1981, placing defense outlays on a path of nearly 9 percent annual real growth between 1981 and 1986. In light of the worsening budget outlook in 1982, the administration adjusted downward its FY 1983 proposals to reflect a slightly lower real growth trend.[4] Congress then adopted a spending resolution for 1983-1985 that was to further reduce defense outlay growth below the president's proposed trend for the three-year period.

The amount by which defense spending has been increased under President Reagan depends entirely upon one's assumption about the anticipated spending pattern under a different administration. As stated earlier, the 5 percent annual real growth planned by President Carter is a plausible alternative assumption for 1982, with growth tapering down to 4 percent in 1983 and 3 percent thereafter. In contrast to this, continuation of President Reagan's requested defense buildup would lead to defense outlays in 1986 that are $69 billion higher. This path of higher defense spending and correspondingly larger deficits throughout the 1982-1986 period also leads net interest outlays to be $11 billion higher than would otherwise be the case. The projected 1986 deficit is thus higher by $80 billion, or 1.9 percent of GNP. Defense outlays would rise under the president's requested buildup from 5.5 percent of GNP in 1981 to 7.7 percent in 1986. The more moderate, alternative growth path would have put defense outlays at 6.1 percent of GNP in 1986 under comparable macroeconomic assumptions.

Changes in Nondefense Program Spending

Nondefense program spending is projected to rise from an estimated level in 1983 of about $525 billion to more than $575 billion in 1986 under current policies. Despite this continued growth, however, annual nondefense program outlays under current policies will be $65 billion lower by 1986 than they would have been if Congress had simply continued the policies in place when President Reagan took office. This reduction amounts to a 10 percent drop from the pre-Reagan baseline estimate for that year. As a percentage of GNP, nondefense programs are now projected to fall from 15.6 percent in 1981 to 13.9 percent in 1986. As significant an achievement as this is for President Reagan, it was less spending restraint than he sought and far less than he needed to control the deficit in the face of the large tax cuts and the defense buildup.

Some categories of nondefense spending, of course, received larger proportional reductions than others. The largest cuts have come in the areas of discretionary federal operations and grants to state and local governments. Under current policies, the projected 1986 funding for such activities will support services at only about three-fourths of their 1981 levels.

The spending category of benefit payments for individuals has received a smaller proportional reduction than the other two categories mentioned above. Within the benefit payments area, programs providing assistance to the low-income population were cut proportionately far greater than others. In social insurance and other non-means-tested benefit programs, there was some modest tightening of eligibility and benefit provisions, including less generous cost-of-living adjustments (COLAs). However, spending for these latter programs still will rise between 1981 and 1986, both in real dollars and as a percentage of GNP. This trend is due in large part to the aging of the population, the increased demands thus placed on health and pension programs, and medical care cost increases that far exceed the general rate of inflation. Increases in these programs account for nearly all the projected growth in nondefense program spending over the period.

Competing Explanations for the Rise in Projected Deficits

Views about the origins of the deficit problem depend upon judgments as to the desirable level of tax burdens, defense capabilities, and the domestic commitments of the federal government. An examination of the Reagan administration's perspective and of competing interpretations of recent budget history illustrates the major points of contention in the present policy debate.

The administration asserts that, the unanticipated recession aside, the projected future deficits are due primarily to the unrestrained growth of nondefense program spending through policies adopted during the 1970s. This argument focuses particularly upon entitlement benefits and the difficulty of reversing their upward momentum. Secondarily, the administration has charged that Congress enacted tax policies that reduce tax burdens beyond the level originally proposed by President Reagan. The administration rejects the claim that the defense buildup is excessive. Indeed, the president has continued to assert that such defense growth is essential to meet the Soviet threat and to insure a strong American bargaining position in arms reduction talks. The principal opposing view is that both the individual income tax cuts in ERTA and the planned defense buildup were excessive and should be scaled back substantially. There is merit to both arguments, as well as contrary evidence.

The revenue loss associated with the individual tax rate reductions and indexing provisions of ERTA does not appear excessive *if* the policy objective was to offset the effects of bracket creep since January 1979. That was the time at which taxpayers first became vulnerable to inflation following the most recent prior adjustment in personal tax rates. To offset the ensuing bracket creep under observed and projected inflation rates would have required individual tax cuts amounting annually to $144 billion by 1986. The rate reductions and indexing provisions of ERTA will yield a 1986 tax cut that is projected to be slightly lower, $133 billion.[5] On the other hand, with the lowering of projected inflation since ERTA's enactment, the 1981 law now provides for a much larger real gain in personal disposable incomes than was originally expected. The three-phased personal rate reductions are now estimated to provide a real tax cut by 1984 that is 65 percent higher than that projected at the time of passage under the previous expectations of stronger inflation.[6]

Before ERTA's passage, concerns were raised over whether the American public would tolerate the rising tax share of GNP that was implied by pre-ERTA policy, or whether the economic incentives necessary for strong economic growth could be sustained in the absence of a large tax cut. The administration answered both questions in the negative. Critics of the administration's tax policy cite international comparisons to counter the proposition that a rising tax burden would inhibit economic growth; U.S. taxes are relatively low when compared with other industrialized nations that have experienced faster growth. Furthermore, they contend that lower tax burdens were simply traded for higher interest rates. The 1981-1982 recession is thus attributed in part to the tax policy changes, as monetary tightening was deemed necessary to contain inflation in the face of the expansionary, supply side fiscal policy. The monetary restraint kept interest rates high and thus adversely affected such sectors as housing, autos, consumer durables, and business investment. For this reason, many judge ERTA to have been irresponsibly large.

The Reagan administration has itself joined in the criticism of ERTA. In early 1983, the administration faulted Congress for enacting provisions in ERTA that "reduced the revenue claim on GNP in 1986-88 by substantially more than was originally proposed."[7] Nevertheless, the White House vigorously supported the 1981 tax bill; indeed, it passed on the strength of the president's endorsement. Granted, such ERTA provisions as indexing and the easing of the marriage penalty had been absent from the administration's legislative proposals of early 1981. Ronald Reagan, however, had proposed indexing as an essential piece of his budget program during the 1980 presidential campaign and indicated after becoming president that the administration would propose both indexing and measures to address the marriage penalty in a subsequent tax package. If one includes these two provisions along with those formally proposed by the Reagan administration in February 1981, the total revenue loss by 1986 would have been virtually the same as that enacted in ERTA.

Whether or not the enacted and planned defense buildup is excessive is a much more ambiguous proposition, given the difficulties in establishing the nature of the threat posed by our foreign adversaries and thus our increased vulnerability to aggressors under more moderate defense growth. The administration argues that its policies simply restore the defense share of GNP by 1988 to 8 percent, still below the peacetime levels that prevailed during the late 1950s and early 1960s. Critics of the defense policy argue that defense needs simply do not require such a high level of spending, that it diverts resources from other problems and priorities, and that the speed of the buildup is so rapid as to prevent a rational procurement strategy and to create supply bottlenecks and inflationary pressures in some industrial sectors.

As mentioned earlier, the administration lays the blame for projected deficits primarily upon continued growth in domestic spending. Projections of current policy show nondefense programs falling to 13.9 percent of GNP by 1986 from their 1981 level of 15.6

percent. This declining GNP share, in the presence of factors such as a growing elderly population that place upward pressures on spending, suggests that considerable spending restraint in domestic programs has in fact been exercised. The administration points out, however, that the projected GNP share of nondefense program spending still far exceeds that attained during the Great Society era of the late 1960s and the subsequent period leading up to the 1974-1975 recession. Also, the GNP share of its dominant component—benefit payments to individuals—is not projected to decline at all from its 1981 level of 11 percent.

This very fact illustrates one of the serious flaws in the administration's budgetary program. Despite the need for a major reduction in the GNP share of nondefense program spending to accommodate the tax cut and defense buildup, the administration did not put forward a coherent strategy to address the future sources of growth in entitlement programs. The president's 1982 budget revisions simply promised, but did not specify, future spending reductions. Under pressure from the Senate, the administration proposed a hastily formulated set of Social Security cuts in May 1981. After these were repudiated by both parties in Congress, the president proposed the creation of a national commission to make recommendations on Social Security financing. Although both Congress and the president were subsequently able to rally around the proposals of this commission and avert the impending trust fund shortfall, the enacted legislation did little to restrain the growth of Social Security benefits over the next several decades. The administration also failed initially to put forward appropriate proposals to restrain the Medicare program. Congress had to order it to submit legislation to contain Medicare hospital costs. In any event the projected savings of the new legislation are modest relative to the expected growth of the Medicare program.

The president's efforts during 1981-1982 to restrain domestic spending were primarily directed at low-income assistance, grants to state and local governments, and discretionary federal operations. Such programs were more politically vulnerable and have in fact been substantially reduced. However, it is the "middle-class entitlements," especially health and pension benefits, that remain the principal sources of domestic spending growth. Here, through its first two years, the administration proposed little in the way of structural reforms that were well designed to achieve the long-term restraint that the administration needed to meet its budgetary objectives.

CHAPTER 4

HOW SERIOUS IS THE DEFICIT PROBLEM?

Projected federal deficits are so large as to endanger the future health of the economy. The government's demands for available credit will likely discourage the levels of private investment necessary to sustain desired rates of long-term economic growth. An immediate program of tax increases and spending reductions, however, might also jeopardize the nation's economic health by curtailing personal consumption and business expenditures. Given these competing concerns, the controversy among experts over the precise economic consequences of deficits, and the role that value judgments must play, there are no hard-and-fast rules as to what constitutes a desirable deficit trend. Budget choices should be based on a careful weighing of the risks of either persistently large deficits or the contractionary fiscal measures by which deficits might be reduced. The indisputable reality is that current policies will lead to unprecedented peacetime deficits, particularly when one abstracts from the cyclical performance of the economy and considers only the structural deficit amount that would remain under high-employment conditions. Although reasonable persons might disagree over the details, it is clearly desirable to phase in a set of substantial deficit reduction measures over the next several years.

The first section of this chapter discusses the extent to which past and projected deficits reflect a fundamental imbalance between tax and spending policies. The reasons for concern over deficits are explored in the second section. Finally, some thoughts are offered on what might constitute a reasonable target for a desired deficit reduction path.

Structural Deficits

Any discussion of the economic consequences of deficits must take account of the rise and fall in economic activity that occurs naturally in the course of the business cycle. Because of the sensitivity of both outlays and revenues to cyclical changes and inflationary trends, even a stable set of tax and spending policies would result in annual changes in the deficit. When the level of economic activity falls off, revenues automatically decline and outlays automatically rise for certain benefit programs, such as unemployment compensation. (Currently, each percentage point rise in the unemployment rate increases the annual deficit by up to $30 billion.)[1] Thus, deficits reflect, as well as influence, the level of economic activity.

One can adjust for these effects of the economy on the budget by computing the annual federal surplus or deficit that would result if the economy were operating at some standardized level. This allows one to isolate the extent to which budget deficits are a result of an underlying imbalance between tax and spending policies, independent of the state of the economy. Year-to-year changes in the standardized deficit measure also indicate the degree of economic stimulus inherent in fiscal policy. The standardized level usually adopted is that associated with high employment, now interpreted as an unemployment rate of about 6 percent. Deficit estimates that are derived using such high-employment assumptions are referred to as "structural deficits."

Over the past two decades, federal structural deficits have consistently ranged below 2 percent of the corresponding standardized GNP level.[2] The notable exception was 1968, when the Vietnam War spending pushed the structural deficit to 4 percent of GNP. The highly stimulative fiscal policy reflected by this increased structural deficit during the Vietnam buildup is thought to be primarily responsible for the acceleration of inflation that began in the late 1960s.

In contrast to this historical pattern, the structural deficit is now projected to grow steadily from 2.9 percent of GNP in 1983 to 5.0 percent in 1988, assuming the president's defense buildup and current tax and nondefense spending policies (table 11). Such deficits would be unprecedented in peacetime. They not only begin at an historically high level, but also grow as a percentage of GNP. Before the policy changes made in 1981, such baseline projections always showed movement toward budget surplus, in large part because of

TABLE 11

THE STRUCTURAL COMPONENT OF PAST AND PROJECTED FEDERAL DEFICITS
(FY 1961–FY 1988)

	Actual					Projected[a]		
	Average							
	FY 1961–FY 1970	FY 1971–FY 1980	FY 1981	FY 1982	FY 1983	FY 1984	FY 1986	FY 1988
	Percentage of GNP[b]							
Total deficit	0.9	2.4	2.7	4.2	7.0	6.0	5.6	5.8
Structural deficit	0.9	1.9	1.2	1.4	2.9	3.2	4.1	5.0
	Billions of Dollars							
Total deficit	—	—	79	128	225	213	236	280
Structural deficit	—	—	37	46	104	123	179	247
(Percentage of total)	—	—	(47)	(36)	(46)	(58)	(76)	(88)

SOURCES: Congressional Budget Office, unpublished CBO tabulations; Office of Management and Budget, "Federal Government Finances," February 1983, pp. 5 and 7; and authors' calculations.

NOTE: All estimates include off-budget outlays, which are assumed not to be cyclically sensitive. Structural deficit projections are standardized at a 6 percent unemployment rate.

a. Estimated under the economic forecast adopted by Congress in passing its *First Concurrent Resolution on the Budget for Fiscal Year 1984.* Assumes adoption of the administration's defense request for FY 1984 and subsequent years, plus the continuation of all tax and spending policies enacted through August 1983 (including the emergency jobs legislation, Social Security amendments, and repeal of tax withholding on interest and dividend income).

b. "Total deficit" estimates are expressed as a percentage of historical or predicted levels of *observed* GNP. "Structural deficit" estimates are expressed as a percentage of *potential* GNP. The reader is cautioned against any interpretation of the difference between the estimated percentages for any given year, due to their differing denominators.

the increase in revenues associated with bracket creep. The scheduled tax reductions enacted through ERTA (including the indexing provisions to be effective in 1985), however, serve to restrain projected revenue growth. In addition, the large increases in real defense spending and interest payments result in faster outlay growth than has been the case in past budget projections.

It must be emphasized that this projected pattern of structural deficits cannot be significantly altered without changes in federal tax and spending policies. Since the measured structural deficit abstracts from the performance of the economy, the assumption of a stronger recovery from the 1981-1982 recession would have little effect on the projected structural deficit trend.[3]

Why Are Deficits Undesirable?

How concerned should we be about such large and growing deficits? Most economists would view as undesirable any large reduction in the deficits confronting us in 1983 and 1984. These near-term deficits are in part a result of the recent recession. Some substantial degree of fiscal stimulus is desirable to sustain the economic recovery. The inflationary risks are small, given the depressed state of the economy (e.g., an unemployment rate of 10 percent and capacity utilization rates in manufacturing just over 70 percent in mid-1983). However, as the economy continues to recover, large and growing deficits become increasingly troublesome. They are likely to have one of two undesirable consequences, conditional in part upon the Federal Reserve's policies and the expectations of the financial community.

On the one hand, the Federal Reserve could accommodate the Treasury's borrowing needs by purchasing federal securities, or "monetizing the debt." This would accelerate the growth of the money supply and, in combination with the very stimulative fiscal policy, might refuel inflation. To hedge against such a risk, creditors would be prompted to keep their long-term interest rates high. The near-term effect would be to weaken those markets sensitive to long-term interest rates, such as housing, and thereby impede economic recovery. The longer-run effect would be to discourage the levels of business investment essential to a high rate of future economic growth.

At the other extreme, the Fed could hold fast to a policy of monetary restraint, seeking to counteract the inflationary pressures posed by strong fiscal stimulus and thus refrain from financing the large federal debt. The federal government would then have to compete with private borrowers for available funds. If the supply of domestic and foreign credit were insufficient to meet both public and private borrowing needs at current interest rates, interest rates would be bid up, and private borrowers would be crowded out. Although the recovery might proceed for several years, the growth of the economy will ultimately be retarded if the credit demands of the government clash substantially with those of the private sector.[4]

The amount of money available for public and private borrowing is primarily determined by the magnitude of net saving in the economy. During 1971-1980 this averaged 8 percent of GNP (table 12). Federal deficits absorbed just over 30 percent of this saving, with the rest available for other investment. From 1981 to 1983, a lower saving rate and larger deficits have led to a rising claim by the federal government on available domestic credit. Only the severely depressed economy and the resulting weak demands of business for funds to finance capital expenditures have prevented a major rise in interest rates.

The Reagan administration had hoped simultaneously to reduce federal borrowing requirements (through a balanced budget) and increase the saving rate (through large business and personal tax cuts). So far the saving rate has not responded favorably. Furthermore, as table 12 demonstrates, the looming federal deficits threaten to reduce substantially the funds available for private investment, even in the face of a rising saving rate. Indeed, current tax and spending policies would leave nonfederal borrowers with domestically available credit that is about one-half as large a percentage of GNP in 1988 as in the 1971-1980 decade (2.9 versus 5.6 percent). More than two-thirds of net saving was available to nonfederal borrowers during the 1971-1980 period, but only one-third of saving would be available for such borrowers in 1988 under projections of current policies. Net inflows of foreign credit might ease the conflict between federal and nonfederal borrowing demands, but it is highly unlikely that a capital infusion of sufficient magnitude to change this basic picture would occur.[5]

Whether the supply of saving will become a constraining factor depends upon business investment plans. As long as capacity utilization is low, businesses have little incentive to increase their capital expenditures. As economic recovery proceeds and production increases, however, businesses will want to expand their capacity.

TABLE 12

FEDERAL DEFICITS AND NET SAVING
(FY 1961–FY 1988)

	Average		Actual			Projected[a]		
	FY 1961– FY 1970	FY 1971– FY 1980	FY 1981	FY 1982	FY 1983	FY 1984	FY 1986	FY 1988
	Billions of Dollars							
Total net domestic saving	56	133	200	206	209	251	352	422
Total deficit	6	42	79	128	225	213	236	280
Remaining amount available for other investment[c]	51	92	121	78	−16	38	116	142
	Percentage of GNP							
Total net domestic saving	7.8	8.0	6.9	6.7	6.5	7.1	8.4	8.7
Total deficit	0.9	2.4	2.7	4.2	7.0	6.0	5.6	5.8
Remaining amount available for other investment[b]	6.9	5.6	4.2	2.5	−0.5	1.1	2.8	2.9

Percentage of Total Net Domestic Saving

Total net domestic savings	100	100	100	100	100	100	100	100
Total deficit	11	31	41	60	108	85	67	66
Remaining amount available for other investment[b]	89	69	59	40	−8	15	33	34

SOURCES: Committee on the Budget, House of Representatives, *First Concurrent Resolution on The Budget—Fiscal Year 1984* (Washington, D.C.: GPO, 1983), p. 33, and unpublished tabulations; authors' calculations.

NOTE: All "total deficit" estimates include off-budget outlays. "Total net domestic saving" is the sum of personal saving, undistributed corporate profits (with inventory valuation and consumption capital adjustments), and state and local government surpluses.

a. Estimated under the economic forecast adopted by the Congress in passing its *First Concurrent Resolution on the Budget for Fiscal Year 1984*. Assumes adoption of the administration's defense request for FY 1984 and subsequent years, plus the continuation of all tax and spending policies enacted through August 1983 (including the emergency jobs legislation, Social Security amendments, and repeal of tax withholding on interest and dividend income).

b. The total amount of credit available for other investment also includes net inflows of foreign credit.

The longer-term deficits are thus much more troublesome than those expected in the next year or so.

Although smaller structural deficits beyond the next few years are likely to promote greater business investment and higher long-term growth, at some point further deficit reductions may no longer be desirable. The financing of government expenditures has implications for the sharing of burdens across generations. Structural deficits shift the costs of higher public spending to subsequent generations through the future taxes needed to finance the public debt, in addition to lowering the long-term growth prospects for the economy. To the extent that future tax-paying generations are the primary beneficiaries of some government expenditures (e.g., for education, preservation of wilderness, research and development, prenatal and infant health care), some forward shift of the financing burden may be appropriate, as long as the displacement of private investment is not excessive.[6] In contrast, the need for deficit reduction is even further heightened under the more extreme view that a *surplus* at high employment may be desirable, if the prospects for future growth could be greatly enhanced by the government's contributing to the pool of available saving. In particular, this may be warranted by virtue of the future obligations being generated under current policies, as with unfunded liabilities in retirement programs.

What Projected Deficit Path Should Be Sought?

If large deficits should be avoided as the economy nears full employment, but if total elimination of the deficit is neither politically possible nor economically imperative, how much deficit reduction should be sought? What criteria can be evoked to guide future tax and spending policies?

As much as policy makers might desire a guideline that would yield a specific target level for future deficits, no standard exists. Nevertheless, the economic context of the present deficit dilemma does suggest something about the desired timing and magnitude of future fiscal actions. First, the economy is moving through a recovery from two back-to-back recessions that left real output no higher in 1982 than in 1979. The short-term impact of tax or spending measures—in conjunction with monetary policy—should not be so severe as to endanger this transition. On the other hand, the structural deficits now projected for the late 1980s would almost certainly interfere with sustained strong economic growth. A five-year budget plan for the 1984-1988 period should thus reflect a progression in the impact of deficit reduction measures from very mild annual impacts in 1984 and 1985 to much more potent effects in 1986 through 1988.

Although some delay in the impact of deficit reduction measures is thus desirable, the possible impact of inflationary expectations on long-term interest rates, and the importance of such rates in promoting housing construction and business investment, means that credible action should be taken now to allay the inflationary fears in the financial community. Such action might also enable the Federal Reserve to adopt a less restrictive monetary posture than it would otherwise pursue.

As indicated earlier, there is no clear-cut target for a five-year deficit reduction plan commencing in 1984. One can devise any number of alternative rules that would dictate a structural deficit ranging from zero to more than 2 percent of standardized GNP. In the presence of such uncertainty, a reasonable goal for current policy action would be to reduce the structural deficit to one percent of GNP by 1988. This is slightly higher than the average structural deficit during the 1960s, but well below the average of the 1970s, a decade that in retrospect appears to have had an overly stimulative fiscal policy.

Under current economic projections, a *structural* deficit target of one percent of standardized GNP translates into a 1988 *total* deficit target of nearly 2 percent of expected GNP. A similar target level has been recently adopted by both liberal and conservative observers.[7] A lowering of the total deficit to 2 percent of GNP by 1988 would also insure a decline by 1988 in the stock of total public debt as a percentage of GNP, an indicator that has recently begun to rise.

Given that current policies imply a 1988 total deficit of 5.8 percent of GNP ($280 billion), a deficit of 2 percent of GNP ($97 billion) would require deficit reduction measures whose annual impact amounts to $183 billion by 1988. Because of the savings in net interest outlays that would result from a progressive pattern of smaller deficits throughout 1984-1988, the sum of revenue increases and program spending reductions must amount annually to over $150 billion by 1988. This figure provides the basis for the discussion in the next chapter of alternative deficit reduction strategies.[8]

CHAPTER 5

STRATEGIES TO REDUCE THE DEFICIT

While the choice of a target level for the federal deficit requires a balancing of economic concerns, the design of a deficit reduction scheme to meet such a prescribed target is primarily a political judgment. The appeal of any plan will depend upon the importance one assigns to limiting the growth of the tax burden, to continuing a buildup of the nation's defense capabilities, and to maintaining the current level of goods, services, and income support provided through federal domestic programs. The need for tradeoffs among these objectives is the essence of the political problem that will continue to confront the president and Congress in seeking to control the deficit. Given the desired magnitude of deficit reduction, the competing alternatives can have dramatic implications for federal tax and spending policies.

The two prevailing deficit reduction strategies—the president's budget and the congressional budget resolution for FY 1984—reflect surprising consensus on the level of revenues, outlays, and the deficit projected for 1988. However, the plans differ considerably on the timing of tax increases and the defense-nondefense mix of program spending. Both fall far short of the prescribed structural deficit target of one percent of GNP. To achieve this target would likely require further concessions on all three deficit reduction fronts: more defense restraint than the president has thus far been willing to accept; greater nondefense program reductions than Congress has thus far been willing to accept; and future tax increases beyond those proposed by either the president or the Congress, since the public seems to want a substantially higher level of public goods and services than current tax policies can finance.

41

Political compromises are necessary if projected deficits are to be substantially reduced, but neither the president nor the Congress appears predisposed to take such action in 1983 or 1984. The risk in forestalling action is that the feasible policy options to reduce the deficits over the period 1986-1988 become increasingly limited.

This chapter first compares the budget plans adopted by the president and Congress for 1984 and subsequent years. It then briefly surveys the opportunities and constraints regarding measures to reduce outlays and increase revenues. The chapter closes with an assessment of the prospects and need for future legislative action.

Fiscal Year 1984 and Beyond: The President's Budget and the Congressional Budget Resolution

President Reagan's FY 1984 budget, proposed to Congress in January 1983, would reduce the 1988 total deficit from a projected $280 billion under current policies to an estimated $159 billion, or 3.3 percent of GNP. The plan would bring the structural deficit down to 2.5 percent of potential GNP, or only part way toward the prescribed one percent target. The administration's proposals include slight tax increases in 1984 and 1985, more substantial revenue gains through a contingency tax plan for the years 1986 through 1988, and further major reductions in nondefense outlays (table 13).

In contrast, the congressional budget resolution for FY 1984, adopted in June 1983, calls for deficit reductions to occur almost entirely through tax increases and defense restraint. It prescribes revenue gains exceeding those recommended by the president for 1984 and 1985, while the 1986 revenue figure is similar to the administration's. The three-year congressional resolution, when extrapolated to 1988, implies a somewhat higher deficit than the president's plan. This results from outlay and revenue totals that are both slightly in excess of the administration's proposal.

The president's plan would boost taxes from their projected 1988 level of 18.7 percent of GNP under current law to 19.9 percent. Of the estimated 1988 revenue increase of $55 billion, about $11 billion would result from a limit on the deductibility of employer-paid health insurance premiums. More importantly, some $40 billion would come through the contingency plan consisting of a surtax equal to 5 percent of individual and corporate tax liabilities and a petroleum excise tax of $5 per barrel. These taxes would be implemented in FY 1986 only if the Congress has accepted the president's proposed nondefense spending cuts, if the administration's mid-1985 economic pro-jections show the FY 1986 budget deficit exceeding 2.5 percent of GNP, and if the economy is still expanding. The provisions would remain effective for no more than three years.

The contingency plan thus seems ill-considered as a serious and permanent deficit reduction proposal. Lifting the provisions after three years, without other subsequent deficit reduction measures already in place, would only serve to subject the economy once again to large and growing structural deficits. Furthermore, the link to enactment of the president's nondefense spending cuts establishes a precondition that, it appears, simply will not be met.

The congressional budget resolution implies a 1988 revenue level of about 20.2 percent of GNP. The specific tax measures are to be proposed by the congressional tax-writing committees.

The president proposed a continuation of his military buildup, with real increases in defense budget authority exceeding 10 percent in 1984 and 11 percent in 1985. In defiance of the president, who indicated a willingness to scale back his requested 1984 growth to 7.5 percent, Congress adopted 5 percent real growth as the basis for its 1984 budget resolution. The precise defense cuts are to be spec-ified by the relevant congressional committees.

While taxes and defense were the most controversial matters in congressional debate over the 1984 budget resolution, it was on nondefense program spending that the president and Congress di-verged most sharply. Neither the House nor the Senate gave serious consideration to the administration's proposed cuts in non-Social Security domestic spending cuts, which were proportionately three-fourths as large as the unprecedented reductions already enacted during 1981-1982. The congressional plan would essentially main-tain nondefense program outlays at the aggregate level implied by current policies for 1988. Even further distancing the congressional budget from the administration's plan was the inclusion by Congress of a temporary reserve fund to support new program initiatives providing antirecession relief and financing physical infrastructure and industrial development. This contingency reserve, available only upon enactment by Congress of authorizing legislation for such ini-tiatives, provides for nearly $14 billion in additional cumulative spending during the years 1984-1986. It seems unlikely to be fully activated, however, particularly as the recovery from the recession grows stronger.

Given the disparity between the executive and legislative bud-get plans, as well as the sensitive political environment for upcoming

TABLE 13

ALTERNATIVE DEFICIT REDUCTION PLANS
(FY 1984–FY 1988)

Billions of Dollars

	Actual, FY 1981	President's Budget			Congressional Resolution[a]		
		FY 1984	FY 1986	FY 1988	FY 1984	FY 1986	FY 1988
Projected total deficit under current policy	—	213	236	280	213	236	280
Deficit reductions	—	−20	−84	−121	−17	−81	−112
Revenue increases[b]	—	−3	−47	−55	−12	−46	−71
Defense outlay reductions	—	0	0	0	−5	−25	−22
Nondefense program outlay reductions	—	−17	−34	−52	1	−3	0
Net interest outlay reductions[c]	—	0	−3	−14	−1	−7	−19
Remaining total deficit	—	193	152	159	196	155	168

Percentage of GNP

Revenues	20.8	18.8	19.9	19.9	19.1	19.8	20.2
Outlays	23.5	24.3	23.5	23.2	24.6	23.5	23.7
Defense	5.5	6.9	7.7	8.1	6.7	7.1	7.6
Nondefense programs	15.6	14.7	13.1	12.6	15.2	13.9	13.7
Net interest	2.4	2.7	2.7	2.4	2.7	2.6	2.3
Total deficit	2.7	5.5	3.6	3.3	5.5	3.7	3.5
Structural deficit	1.2	2.7	2.2	2.5	2.8	2.3	2.7

SOURCES: Congressional Budget Office, unpublished tabulations; authors' calculations.

NOTE: Deficit reduction plans estimated under the economic forecast adopted by the Congress in passing its *First Concurrent Resolution on the Budget for Fiscal Year 1984*. Assumes adoption of the administration's defense request for FY 1984 and subsequent years, plus the continuation of all tax and spending policies enacted through August 1983 (including the emergency jobs legislation, Social Security amendments, and repeal of tax withholding on interest and dividend income).

a. Does not include the antirecession reserve, a contingency fund that might result in additional cumulative outlays of nearly $14 billion during the years 1984–1986. The 1988 projection is based upon CBO extrapolations of the initial House and Senate versions of the budget resolution.

b. For 1986 and 1988, about $40 billion of the president's proposed revenue increases would result from contingency measures becoming effective in 1986 only if conditions are met regarding nondefense spending reductions, the projected size of the deficit, and the rate of economic growth. These revenue measures would remain in effect only through 1988.

c. For the president's budget, the savings in net interest outlays owing to lower deficits is partly offset by a reduction in intra-governmental interest collections, resulting from proposed policy changes in various federal credit activities.

budgetary decisions, what are the prospects for improvement in the deficit outlook? With respect to congressional action throughout 1984, a pessimistic—but plausible—scenario is that the deficit projected under policies in effect up to September 1983 will remain materially unaffected. Neither the president, the House Democratic leadership, nor the Senate Republican leadership wields sufficient power to command support for any serious attack on the deficit. The severity of the problem and the need for compromise is widely acknowledged. Yet any national leader wishing to strike a bipartisan agreement must engage in a dangerous form of double jeopardy. An elected official risks attack from political rivals by seeking concessions on some issues, while perhaps weakening his or her bargaining position by offering concessions on other matters. Without President Reagan's endorsement, Congress will find it hard even to implement the policies prescribed by its own 1984 budget resolution, most particularly the tax increases.

Even if the factions within Congress could agree upon measures to carry out the spending and revenue targets in the congressional resolution, the president has threatened to veto any bills that exceed his own proposals with respect to either revenue increases in 1984-1985 or nondefense spending levels. The president's disdain for tax increases before 1986 may endanger the chances for enactment of revenue gains thereafter, especially since base-broadening measures and other tax provisions must often be phased in gradually. Although a series of presidential vetoes on domestic discretionary spending bills might lead to a temporary freeze on program funding at 1983 levels, the savings by 1988 of even a two-year, across-the-board freeze on such spending would be less than $10 billion. Beyond this, the only appreciable nondefense spending cuts may come through federal pay restraint, a delay in retirement COLAs, and lower farm price supports. The 1988 impact of such action would not exceed $10 billion, and even these savings might be forgone if packaged in the same legislation as the tax changes.

The president may have to accept more short-term restraint in defense budget authority than he considers prudent, but significant long-term outlay reductions will occur only if Congress repeatedly adopts lower real growth in budget authority in the course of its annual appropriations process. If the defense restraint is exercised only for one year, the 1988 savings is once again less than $10 billion. These points simply illustrate that budgetary developments through early 1985 could easily leave the projected 1988 total deficit above

$200 billion, with the structural deficit remaining above $150 billion (or more than 3 percent of potential GNP).

Even if Congress were to implement the provisions of its budget resolution, the long-term deficit outlook would not be particularly bright. Measured against a structural deficit target of one percent of GNP by 1988, both the congressional budget and the president's plan fall well short of sufficient deficit reduction. Even if Congress were to adopt the full amount of nondefense spending restraint proposed by the president in addition to its tax increases and defense restraint, the target would not be achieved. In any event, the present congressional mood runs strongly counter to such large additional domestic budget cuts. Thus, if very large deficits are not to persist, Congress not only must move somewhat closer to the president's position on domestic spending restraint but also must consider higher tax increases and perhaps more defense restraint than its budget resolution now specifies. Such action on the tax and defense fronts would put Congress even further at odds with the president.

This clash in political preferences currently appears to jeopardize hope for a significant lowering of projected structural deficits. Concern over the potential impact of these deficits on the economy, however, may yet force the president and Congress to reconsider their positions.

Opportunities and Prospects for Deficit Reduction

Any plan to reduce the deficit must reckon with political realities and the inexorable dynamics of federal taxes and spending. How do these forces constrain budgetary choices? What are some of the more specific tradeoffs confronting policy makers who seek to control the deficit?

Restraining Nondefense Program Spending. Nondefense program spending stood at 15.6 percent of GNP when President Reagan took office and would have declined somewhat by 1988 had there been no changes in the policies he inherited. As a result of budget reductions to date, however, this spending is now projected to decline markedly to 13.7 percent of GNP by 1988. In his 1984 budget, the president proposed substantial additional reductions in nondefense program spending that would lower it by another 1.1 percent of GNP to 12.6 percent by 1988. In contrast the congressional budget resolution for 1984 did not prescribe any further overall domestic reductions. To consider the opportunities and constraints for further cuts in nondefense program spending, it is useful to examine at a somewhat more disaggregated level the current policy projections as well as the pending budget proposals of the president and Congress.

President Reagan has proposed a wide-ranging set of deficit reduction measures that are significant for all major categories of

TABLE 14

NONDEFENSE PROGRAM OUTLAYS—PROJECTED GROWTH AND THE
PRESIDENT'S PROPOSED REDUCTIONS
(FY 1983–FY 1988)

	Projected Outlays Under Current Policy[a]			President's Proposed Reductions in FY 1988 Outlays, Relative to Current Policy Projection
	FY 1983	FY 1988	Change	
	Billions of Dollars			
Entitlements and other mandatory spending	392	507	115	−16
Social Security	169	228	59	0
Medicare	56	106	50	−5
Other retirement and disability[b]	40	53	13	−2
Major means-tested programs[c]	52	69	17	−2
Farm price supports	22	19	−13	−3
Other[d]	53	42	−11	−4
Discretionary spending	146	183	37	−20
Benefits and services to individuals	48	58	10	−9
Infrastructure, research and development	58	71	13	−8
Assistance to business and commerce	8	10	2	−5
Other[e]	32	44	12	2[f]
Offsetting receipts	−32	−40	−8	−8

TABLE 14 (continued)

| | Projected Outlays Under Current Policy[a] | | | President's Proposed Reductions in FY 1988 Outlays, Relative to Current Policy Projection |
	FY 1983	FY 1988	Change	
Medicare premiums	−4	−7	−3	−4
Other[g]	−28	−33	−5	−4
Off-budget spending	18	16	−2	−8
Farm insurance	4	5	1	−5
Other[h]	14	11	−3	−3
TOTAL	524	665	141	−52

SOURCES: Congressional Budget Office, *An Analysis of the President's Budgetary Proposals for Fiscal Year 1984* (Washington, D.C.: GPO, 1983), and unpublished CBO tabulations.

a.   Estimated under the economic forecast adopted by the Congress in passing its *First Concurrent Resolution on the Budget for Fiscal Year 1984.* Assumes adoption of the administration's defense request for FY 1984 and subsequent years, plus the continuation of all spending policies enacted through August 1983 (including the emergency jobs legislation and Social Security amendments of 1983).

b.   Primarily Civil Service retirement, railroad retirement, and veterans' compensation.

c.   Aid to Families with Dependent Children, child support enforcement, Food Stamps, Supplemental Security Income, veterans' pensions, and Medicaid.

d.   The largest programs in this category are unemployment compensation, general revenue sharing, social services, child nutrition, and guaranteed student loans.

e.   Includes federal government operations and international assistance.

f.   This increase largely represents higher contributions by federal agencies to the civil service retirement fund, which also appear as higher offsetting receipts.

g.   Primarily the rents and royalties from off-shore oil operations, the proceeds from sale or lease of other mineral and timber resources, and the receipts from federal agencies of employer contributions for civil service retirement and health benefits.

h.   The largest programs in this category are the strategic petroleum reserve, the Postal Service, and federal credit funds to support rural electrification and foreign military sales.

spending and offsetting receipts, with the exception of Social Security (table 14). Consistent with the pattern of prior reductions, he is advocating much larger proportional cuts in discretionary spending than in the entitlements and other mandatory spending. The largest discretionary reductions would come in benefits and services—such as housing, education, social services, health, employment, and training—intended primarily for the low-income population. This is the same category of programs that has been most severely cut thus far. Unlike the previous pattern, however, the president's proposed reductions in entitlements and other mandatory spending are not concentrated among those providing assistance to low-income population but are largely in the so-called middle-class programs.

The unwillingness of Congress to reduce nondefense program spending any further in its 1984 budget resolution indicates the political difficulties that lie ahead for any general deficit reduction scheme that attempts to rely substantially upon this component of the budget. The congressional resolution calls for some modest reductions in certain areas—most notably federal pay, farm price supports, and Medicare. However, it also prescribes some offsetting *increases* above current policy levels concentrated in discretionary benefits and services to individuals—the very area where the president desires to cut the most. This presumably reflects the widely noted sentiment in Congress and the general public that programs serving the low-income population have already borne enough, if not too much, of the burden of spending restraint. (This discussion excludes consideration of the contingency reserve fund. Were that to be activated, congressional nondefense spending would temporarily rise above the currently projected levels.)

The current policy projections in table 14 illustrate the difficulty of reducing nondefense spending without acting significantly on entitlements and other mandatory spending. Such programs comprise three-fourths of nondefense program spending. Social Security and Medicare alone comprise nearly one-half of nondefense program spending and, despite the recently enacted legislation reducing their outlay growth, are projected to account for over three-fourths of the nondefense program growth over the next five years. To reduce the 1988 structural deficit to the desired level by relying substantially on nondefense spending restraint, but without large further reductions in Social Security and Medicare, implies drastic reductions in other nondefense programs—well beyond what Congress and the public appear willing to support. The overall contribution of nondefense spending cuts will be marginal at best if limited to modest reductions in the other middle-class entitlement and mandatory spending programs and the various discretionary programs not targeted on the low-income population. The need to take action to avert the large deficits that are projected for the Medicare program beginning in the late 1980s offers one prospect for major additional entitlement restraint. However, Congress is unlikely to act on this for several years.

Scaling Back the Defense Buildup. The opportunities to re-strain defense outlays are severely limited in the short run by the magnitude of present spending that results from prior years' contracts and obligations. Over one-third of FY 1983's defense outlays flow from previously enacted budget authority. Under the president's budget, with its emphasis on weapons procurement and other long-term military commitments, defense spending will become even less subject to short-term restraint; by 1988, 43 percent of defense outlays would result from prior budget authority.[1] If one adds to this the 5 percent of defense outlays that constitute military retirement benefits, nearly one-half of the projected defense budget would be virtually beyond any immediate control.

Any discussion of defense restraint must therefore be cast in terms of a sustained, multiyear reduction in the rate of growth of budget authority enacted by Congress through its annual defense appropriations. The president's plan calls for real growth in defense budget authority at an annual rate of about 7 percent during the 1984-1988 period, with growth exceeding 10 percent in 1984 and 1985 but diminishing substantially thereafter to less than 4 percent.[2] As mentioned earlier, the congressional budget resolution now calls for 5 percent annual real growth. Each sustained percentage point reduction in this growth rate results in an annual outlay savings of only $1 billion in the first year, but $12 to $13 billion by the fifth year. The impact on the deficit of such congressional action thus comes with a considerable lag. Stated otherwise, any serious attempt to restrain outlays within the next five years must be initiated now. If successfully implemented, the current congressional plan would yield an estimated $22 billion in outlay savings by 1988, compared to the president's budget. An even more ambitious scheme, one allowing real growth in budget authority of 5 percent in 1984 and 1985, but only 3 percent thereafter, would save about $33 billion from the administration's request for 1988.

Excluding the costs of military retirement, the defense budget can be divided into military operations (the payroll for active duty civilian and military personnel, plus other operations and maintenance costs) and military investment (procurement of weaponry and equipment, construction of facilities, and research and development). Military operations now comprise 55 percent of defense outlays. This amount, along with the portion of procurement associated with spare parts, support equipment, and munitions, sustains the readiness of our defense forces. The remaining military investment outlays promote the modernization of our defense capabilities. It is the latter type of spending that is the principal source of growth in the administration's defense budget, projected to nearly double in real terms between 1981 and 1986. It is also the most politically difficult to restrain, requiring that specific weapons purchases be stretched out, scaled back, or simply canceled.

The difficulty of exercising restraint on weapons procurement has led Congress in the past to seek savings through reduced funding for readiness needs. As a long-term strategy, however, this can only lead to weaker defense capabilities than could have been purchased otherwise. Personnel would be more poorly trained and equipped. The physical plant of ships, missiles, aircraft, armored vehicles, and other combat hardware, while perhaps reflecting state-of-the-art technology, would be more poorly maintained and thus less able to respond when needed.

While the degree of defense restraint that the Congress has now adopted in its budget resolution may appear modest, it will be very difficult to achieve. Of the estimated $22 billion in 1988 savings, $3 billion can be attained through the 4 percent limit on annual pay increases called for in the resolution; an additional $1 billion will come from the prescribed six-month delay in the military retirement COLA. It seems prudent to seek the remaining $18 billion primarily through restraint on weapons modernization, rather than a contin-ued weakening of military readiness. Illustrative of the difficulty of achieving such a target, however, is that the savings associated with scaleback or cancellation of eight major weapons systems, including cancellation of the MX missile, would amount to less than $11 billion by 1988.[3] This suggests that achieving the congressional target will require considerable restraint on both readiness and modernization spending, through fewer units purchased and greater efficiency in the procurement process.[4] Nevertheless, it seems unlikely that Con-gress could achieve defense savings much in excess of those implied by the present budget resolution.

Tax Increases. Outlays under current policies and the presi-dent's requested defense buildup are projected to be 24.5 percent of GNP in 1988. Lowering this level to 23 percent would require a total of $30 billion of savings through some combination of nondefense program cuts and a further scaling back of the defense buildup beyond that ($22 billion) prescribed in the budget resolution. The political support necessary to achieve this large a reduction in public goods and services, let alone a greater one, is not now evident. Given this difficulty, a target total deficit of 2 percent of GNP implies that 1988 revenues might have to rise to at least 21 percent of GNP, or virtually the same percentage as in 1981. Since current tax policies are projected to yield 1988 revenues of 18.7 percent of GNP, a 21 percent tax burden implies tax increases that by 1988 amount to 2.3 percent of GNP, or over $100 billion. The set of revenue measures to achieve such a tax boost would have to be selected with a host of considerations in mind, including distributional impacts and incentives to work, save, and invest. In addition, pragmatic political judgments may suggest that some alternatives are simply infeasible.

The potential need for such large future revenue increases has led to consideration of major structural reforms to the federal tax system that would broaden the tax base, relate tax liabilities more to consumption rather than income or wealth, and simplify the schedule of tax rates. Such proposals include replacing the current individual income tax with a flat-rate income tax or a broad-based consumption tax, or the imposition of a new national sales tax (or value-added tax). Most flat-rate options would maintain some progressivity in individual tax rates but would enable lower marginal rates than currently exist by repealing virtually all itemized deductions and exclusions. A consumption tax would make individual tax liabilities a function of personal expenditures, calculated as the difference between income and saving. Likewise, a value-added tax would discourage consumption and encourage saving, since the tax would be passed along to consumers through price increases.

While such wholesale tax reforms offer the prospect of higher revenues, improved economic incentives, and some simplification of the tax system, they raise serious political, administrative, and distributional problems. With no apparent groundswell of public support or bipartisan political backing to counter the expected opposition from a multitude of adversely affected groups, these reform strategies do not appear to offer significant potential for additional revenues within the five-year time frame discussed here.

If the necessary revenue increases are not likely to come through sweeping tax changes, what revisions to the existing tax code might be enacted? It seems inevitable that a series of different revenue measures ultimately will be required, spreading the burden of additional taxes broadly across individuals and businesses. Such changes will most likely take the form of some increase in tax rates for individual or corporate income taxes, some broadening of the taxable base for both personal and business-related income, and some higher

TABLE 15

INCREASE IN FEDERAL REVENUES UNDER SELECTED TAX MEASURES
(FY 1988)

	Billions of Dollars
Rate Increases	
Delay indexing of individual income tax	40
Surtax on individual and corporate income tax liabilities (5 percent)	20[a]
Base-broadening measures in individual income tax	
Limit deductibility of employer-paid health insurance premiums	11[a]
Eliminate deductibility of consumer interest payments	10
Limit deductibility of home mortgage interest to $5,000	9
Tax accrued interest on life insurance reserves	9
Eliminate deductibility of state and local sales taxes	8
Tax selected entitlement benefits[b]	8
Eliminate income averaging	5
Base-broadening measures in business-related taxes	
Lengthen building depreciation period to 20 years	8
Require full basis adjustment for investment tax credit	5
Repeal expensing of intangible drilling costs for oil and gas	4
Energy consumption taxes	
Broad-based tax on domestic energy (5 percent)	22
Excise tax on domestic and imported petroleum (5 dollars per barrel)	21[a]
Excise taxes on gasoline (increased by 5 cents per gallon) and natural gas (30 cents per 1000 cubic feet)	7
Other excise taxes	
Double excise taxes on alcohol and cigarettes	6
Extend excise tax on telephone service	3

SOURCES: Congressional Budget Office, *Analysis of the President's Budgetary Proposals for Fiscal Year 1984* (Washington, D.C.: GPO, 1983), pp. 26–27, and *Reducing the Deficit: Spending and Revenue Options* (Washington, D.C.: GPO, 1983), pp. 234, 250–251, 253, 258, and 263.

a. Included in the revenue proposals of the president's budget for FY 1984. The income surtax and petroleum excise tax comprised the president's "contingency tax plan."

b. Assumes taxation of 40 percent of railroad retirement benefits and the full amount of benefits from workers' compensation, unemployment insurance, and veterans' disability compensation.

excise taxes, especially on energy. (See table 15 for illustrative examples.) In the realm of political feasibility, there simply exists no small set of tax increases that yields a total annual revenue gain as large as $100 billion by 1988. For example, a surtax of 10 percent on personal income tax liabilities (twice as large as in the president's contingency tax plan) or a delay in the indexing of the individual income tax, in combination with an energy consumption tax equivalent to the one the president has proposed, would yield just over $60 billion in 1988. Thus an additional $40 billion would have to be raised through other means, such as a variety of base-broadening measures that would each face vigorous interest group opposition.

There would be strong political resistance to near-term increases in Social Security taxes, given that the recently enacted reforms included an acceleration of scheduled payroll tax increases in addition to other financing measures. The Medicare trust fund, however, will be bankrupt by the end of the 1980s if steps are not taken to restrain further its benefit growth and raise its revenues. Thus, it would be prudent for some portion of the tax increases between now and 1988 to be related to this program.

The particular selection of revenue-raising measures must strike a balance between policy objectives that often conflict, even in the context of particular proposals: surtaxes may be distributionally neutral, but they necessarily raise marginal tax rates and thus discourage work and saving; excise taxes on energy or other goods serve to encourage saving, but they typically fall most heavily on the low-income population. While base-broadening proposals provoke strong interest group opposition, they would not increase marginal tax rates and would remove the preferential treatment now accorded on questionable grounds to particular forms of economic activity. Just as direct outlay programs have been subject to close scrutiny in the search for spending restraint, so should the tax expenditures that we incur through such limitations to taxable income. These special subsidies are much less defensible in light of the compelling national interests at stake in the search for additional revenue.

A Concluding Assessment

While few would dispute that a phased reduction in the federal deficit enhances the long-term prospects for the U.S. economy, there is no consensus about how to reduce the deficit. In seeking tax increases or spending cuts, politicians must ask voters to accept personal economic sacrifices when the presumed long-term gains for the national economy have uncertain consequences for any particular constituency. Without concerted bipartisan action between the president and the Congress, any official wishing to exercise fiscal statesmanship must accept great risk to his or her own political future.

Under these circumstances, it is tempting for politicians to view the deficit as an issue that will go away under a strong economy. Unfortunately, any upward revisions in the strength of the anticipated recovery from the 1981-1982 recession will reduce only slightly the need for deliberate policy action. Present tax and spending policies embody so large a structural disparity between revenues and outlays that, even if one assumes that the economy could speedily achieve its high-employment potential, the deficit would remain well above any peacetime precedent.

Although economic concerns do not suggest the need for major reductions in the projected deficits for 1984 and 1985, this does not mean that the legislative actions themselves should be delayed. To the contrary, the budgetary measures necessary to achieve a progressive pattern of deficit reduction should be taken soon for several reasons.

First, the high political risks that officials face in supporting tax increases and spending cuts will only grow as the 1984 elections approach. Second, tax increases must often be phased in gradually in order to be politically acceptable and in order not to abruptly alter the economic conditions facing individuals and firms. This is especially true of base-broadening proposals, which provoke intense opposition from adversely affected interest groups. Third, defense spending has a built-in momentum through previous contractual commitments for weapons procurement. If future outlays are to be reduced, decisions must be made now as to which weapons purchases should be stretched out or canceled. If these decisions are not made now and if Congress later seeks prompt reductions in defense outlays, the only recourse will be to weaken the readiness of our existing military forces through reductions in spending for operations and maintenance. Such tradeoffs between military readiness and modernization tend to weaken defense capabilities more than an orderly scaleback in some combination of these expenditures. Finally, any limit to the inflationary adjustments in either entitlement or discretionary domestic spending programs will yield appreciable savings only if sustained over several years. And more basic structural changes in entitlement programs often yield savings only very slowly or need to be deliberately phased in over many years in order to ease their potential adverse impacts.

What do these observations on the timing of legislative action and budgetary impacts suggest about a particular five-year scheme of deficit reduction measures? Bearing in mind that a prudent objective would be to enact explicit measures yielding at least $150 billion in deficit reduction by 1988, the political constraints and budgetary dynamics imply that a mix of measures to increase taxes and reduce spending will be necessary. The limited prospects for spending restraint mean that two-thirds or more of the $150 billion amount may have to come through higher revenues. The need to rely so heavily on tax increases is only further heightened if no significant further action is taken to restrain outlay growth in Social Security and Medicare. Any other strategy implies drastic reductions in other nondefense programs.

To go further in outlining a deficit reduction plan would require more detailed policy judgments, with the following considerations in mind. To the extent that tax increases are to occur, the equity and efficiency of our present tax system seem best preserved by relying as much as possible on base-broadening measures rather than on tax rate increases. To the extent that defense outlays are to be restrained, it can be argued that our defense capabilities are best preserved through a scaleback of future weapons purchases rather than through a reduced commitment to current readiness. To the extent that the growth in domestic spending is cut, middle-class entitlements will need to be scrutinized.

Since tax increases and spending reductions impose collective sacrifices on the American public, with some groups inevitably being affected more adversely than others, the policy judgments are appropriately political ones. As suggested by the foregoing discussion, the choices are indeed difficult, and will sorely test the political courage of our elected officials. The abiding economic interests require that the president and members of Congress resist the temptation to take political advantage of those who step forward to support fiscally responsible, but politically unpopular, budgetary policies.

NOTES

NOTES TO CHAPTER 2

1. The terms baseline, baseline projection, and current policy projection are used throughout this book in discussing the impact of policy changes on federal revenues and outlays. Those terms simply refer to the expected path of revenues or outlays in the absence of policy changes. This path forms the standard by which to isolate the effect of the policy changes themselves, as distinct from economic conditions, demographic trends, or other factors influencing budgetary outcomes. An estimated reduction in outlays "relative to a baseline projection" is thus a reduction in the amount of expected spending growth that would otherwise have occurred. The liability of such estimates is that they must rely upon judgments about future circumstances that are subject to great uncertainty.

2. The contribution of inflation to revenue growth was estimated from Frank de Leeuw and Thomas M. Holloway, "The High-Employment Budget: Revised Estimates and Automatic Inflation Effects," *Survey of Current Business*, April 1982, pp. 21-33.

3. The taxable earnings base was nearly doubled, from $15,300 in 1976 to $29,700 in 1981, and the combined employee-employer payroll tax rate jumped from 11.7 to 13.3 percent.

4. Assume all income to have been taxable, with itemized deductions equal to 23 percent of income.

5. See Charles R. Hulten and June A. O'Neill, "Tax Policy," chapter 4 in John L. Palmer and Isabel V. Sawhill (eds.), *The Reagan Experiment* (Washington, D.C.: The Urban Institute, 1982), p. 105.

6. *Ibid.*, p. 104, and authors' calculations of the Social Security payroll tax. This rising tax burden reflected not only bracket creep and payroll tax increases, but also a rising standard of living. Over this twenty-year period, the purchasing power represented by the median income increased by more than one-third.

7. The family is assumed to use the standard deduction.

8. *Ibid.*, p. 105. The upper-income family is assumed to itemize its deductions.

9. However, the 1961-1981 period was marked by four separate eras in defense spending. From 1961 to 1966, inflation-adjusted outlays remained stable at the post-Korean War level that had prevailed throughout the late 1950s. The Vietnam War buildup from 1966 to 1968 then increased real outlays by one-third. This was followed by a steady decline through 1976 in real defense spending, to a level below that of the late 1950s and early 1960s. That trend was then reversed during the 1976-1981 period, with outlays once again reaching their post-Korean War level.

10. Congressional Budget Office, *Defense Spending and the Economy* (Washington, D.C.: Government Printing Office (GPO), 1983), p. 2.

11. Estimates in this section exclude interest outlays necessary to finance the public debt but include the modest amount of off-budget program spending. Off-budget outlays are excluded from the federal budget by statutory provision but must be financed through tax revenues or government borrowing, as with on-budget spending. The off-budget outlays are associated largely with the credit operations of the Federal Financing Bank, for such activities as rural electrification, agriculture credit insurance, rural farm housing, and foreign military sales.

12. Most programs were explicitly indexed to a measure of price change. Health financing programs such as Medicare and Medicaid, though not explicitly indexed, experienced more rapid growth than the general rate of inflation because they absorbed the even faster escalating costs of medical care through their cost reimbursement schedules.

13. One should note that the economic projections of the administration were predicated on the assumption that its budget policies would be adopted.

14. See Congressional Budget Office, *Baseline Budget Projections: Fiscal Years 1982-1986* (Washington, D.C.: GPO, 1981), pp. 28, 29. The Congressional Budget Office (CBO) is the principal source of budgetary projections cited in this book. Without the assumed adjustment for bracket creep, revenues would have risen to 22.9 percent of GNP by 1986. Ibid, p. xiv.

15. Congress does not directly control outlays but rather appropriates budget authority to federal agencies. This authority to make spending commitments does not result in outlays until the Treasury actually disburses funds, such as through payroll checks to federal employees or payments to federal contractors. In national defense spending, budget authority enacted in one year may not result in outlays until several years later, as in the case of long-term weapons procurement. A rising pattern of budget authority must eventually translate into higher outlays. FY 1981 appropriations for national defense amounted to a 25 percent increase in budget authority from the prior year, with no adjustment for inflation. See Office of Management and Budget, "Federal Government Finances," February 1983, p. 58.

NOTES TO CHAPTER 3

1. The budget story from January 1981 to September 1983 can be told in numerous ways. This chapter examines the shifting budget outlook as affected by both substantive policy changes and economic conditions. The magnitude of revenues, outlays, and the deficit are thus the principal focus. Alternatively, one could dwell upon the process within the administration and the Congress by which economic programs and budget policies were developed and enacted. One can argue, indeed, that an important legacy of budgetary action thus far under President Reagan will be its future impact on the way our political institutions arrive at budgetary decisions. Nonetheless, the numbers themselves are critical to the tenor of the public debate and will set the constraints for policy action.

2. Safe harbor leasing rules allow the transfer from unprofitable to profitable companies of unused investment tax credits and depreciation deductions.

3. The withholding requirement for interest and dividend income was repealed in 1983. The revenue estimates reported here for TEFRA have been adjusted to reflect this subsequent action.

4. Office of Management and Budget, "Federal Government Finances," March 1981 edition (p. 75) and February 1982 edition (p. 69).

5. Congressional Budget Office, *Reducing the Deficit: Spending and Revenue Options* (Washington, D.C.: GPO, 1983) p. 238.

Notes 61

6. Committee on the Budget, House of Representatives, *First Concurrent Resolution on The Budget—Fiscal Year 1984* (Washington, D.C.: GPO, 1983), p. 80.
7. Office of Management and Budget, *Budget of the United States Government, Fiscal Year 1984*, January 1983, p. 3-19.

NOTES TO CHAPTER 4

1. See Office of Management and Budget, *The Budget of the U.S. Government, Fiscal Year 1984*, January 1983, p. 2-24, and Congressional Budget Office, *The Economic and Budget Outlook: An Update* (Washington, D.C.: GPO, 1982), p. 91.
2. Standardized GNP, when estimated under high-employment conditions, is commonly referred to as potential GNP. Consistent with CBO projections, potential real output is assumed here to grow annually by 2.6 percent, keeping pace with productivity increases and growth in the labor force so as to maintain the unemployment rate at its high-employment level.
3. A stronger recovery might result in a slightly lower projected level of the structural deficit, for two reasons. First, interest outlays would be somewhat lower, since the cyclical component of the total deficit would decline more rapidly. (By convention, structural deficit estimates assume interest outlays to be based upon the projected path of the *total* deficit through the preceding year.) Second, the higher rate of inflation that is likely to accompany a faster recovery would shift high-employment revenues upward by more than the upward shift in high-employment outlays, even with indexing in place after 1985. If annual real growth can be sustained at a rate that is 0.5 percentage point above the currently projected trend, the 1988 structural deficit would be reduced from its presently estimated level by about $25 billion, or 0.5 percent of potential GNP.
4. Another consequence of the high U.S. interest rates resulting from either future scenario would be to support the currently high exchange value of the U.S. dollar, with foreigners seeking investments in this country. While this capital influx would increase the total supply of credit, a strong dollar makes American-produced goods more expensive to foreigners and makes foreign products less expensive to Americans. Such conditions would continue to place at a disadvantage those U.S. companies relying on export trade or those facing import competition.
5. During 1979-1982, with very high U.S. interest rates to attract foreign capital, such sources supplied only 8 percent of federal borrowing from the public. See Office of Management and Budget, "Special Analysis E—Borrowing and Debt," *Special Analyses, Budget of the United States Government, Fiscal Year 1984* (Washington, D.C.: GPO, 1983), p. E-13.
6. The absence of a separate federal budget for capital expenditures makes it difficult to assess the magnitude of such expenditures. For a discussion of the level of federal investment-type outlays, see Office of Management and Budget, "Special Analysis D—Investment, Operating, and Other Federal Outlays," *Special Analyses, Budget of the United States Government, Fiscal Year 1984* (Washington, D.C.: GPO, 1983), pp. D-1 through D-24.
7. Policy analysts differ on the timing of attainment of this deficit target of 2 percent of GNP. Among the more ambitious of recent plans is the "Bipartisan Appeal to Resolve the Budget Crisis," which proposes a target level of 2 percent of GNP for the FY 1985 deficit. This plan, spearheaded by former Commerce Secretary Peter Peterson and former Treasury Secretaries Blumenthal, Connally, Dillon, Fowler, and Simon, has been endorsed by numerous business leaders, academicians, and former public officials. See "To the President and Congress: A Bipartisan Appeal to Resolve the Budget Crisis," *Wall Street Journal*, January 25, 1983, pp. 40-41. Economists at the American Enterprise Institute for Public Policy Research have adopted 2 percent of GNP as the deficit target for FY 1987. See Philip Cagan, William Fellner, Rudolph Penner, and Herbert Stein, "Economic Policy for Recovery and Growth," *The AEI*

Economist, December 1982, p. 506. The National Governors' Association, in its deficit reduction plan endorsed in March 1983, proposed a 2 percent target for FY 1988. See "Governors Ask U.S. to Reduce Deficit in Federal Budget," *New York Times,* March 2, 1983, pp. A1 and A23. The Congressional Budget Office, in discussing deficit reduction strategies, has used the 2 percent of GNP deficit target for 1988 as an intermediate estimate from among current views in the fiscal policy debate. See Congressional Budget Office, *Reducing the Deficit: Spending and Revenue Options* (Washington, D.C.: GPO, 1983), p. 18. Finally, the Brookings Institution has used 0 to 1 percent of GNP as a target range for the 1988 *structural* deficit. This implies a 1988 *total* deficit of about 1.5-2.5 percent of GNP, given the Brookings estimate of the cyclical deficit component in 1988. See Joseph A. Pechman (ed.), *Setting National Priorities: The 1984 Budget* (Washington, D.C.: Brookings Institution, 1983), pp. 33 and 217. All of the above estimates exclude off-budget outlays.

8. This assumes the annual deficit reductions during 1984-1988 to be as follows (in billions of dollars excluding net interest savings): 15, 40, 70, 105, and 150. A steadily increasing pattern of deficit reductions, one *not* weighted more heavily toward the latter years, would exhibit the following progression: 30, 60, 90, 120, and 150.

NOTES TO CHAPTER 5

1. Congressional Budget Office, *An Analysis of the President's Budgetary Proposals for Fiscal Year 1984* (Washington, D.C.: GPO, 1983), p. 85.

2. The eventual decline in growth under the president's request does not reflect a reduced commitment to the defense buildup as much as it stems from the practice of including only the budget authority associated with military purchases that can now be explicitly identified. As new weapons systems are developed, the future budget authority requested by the administration presumably would exceed the levels now cited in the president's plan.

3. Congressional Budget Office, *Reducing the Deficit: Spending and Revenue Options* (Washington, D.C.: GPO, 1983), pp. 38-52 and 322-323. The specific actions (and their corresponding outlay savings in 1988) are as follows:

—cancel the F/A-18 attack bomber to be deployed by the Navy and Marine Corps, and substitute the cheaper A-6E aircraft ($1.9 billion);

—cancel the Army's Division Air Defense Gun (DIVAD), developed to attack helicopters and other low-flying enemy aircraft ($0.5 billion);

—cancel the Army's Scout surveillance helicopter and rely upon the existing OH-58 helicopter ($0.4 billion);

—cancel the MX missile, a land-based intercontinental ballistic missile designed to survive a Soviet first strike, and rely upon the submarine-launched Trident II missile ($4.0 billion);

—reduce the purchase of the Air Force's F-15 fighter aircraft from a proposed annual rate of 96 by 1986 to only 30 ($2.3 billion);

—limit the re-engining of the Strategic Air Command's KC-135 tanker aircraft used for aerial refueling ($0.2 billion);

—cancel nine of the Navy's DDG-51-class destroyers and substitute with three CG-47-class cruisers ($0.5 billion); and

—cancel the Air Force's C-17 transport aircraft designed for tactical rapid deployment ($0.9 billion).

4. Numerous examples of inefficiencies in defense contracting were recently identified through President Reagan's "Private Sector Survey on Cost Control." This effort to find governmentwide opportunities for federal cost savings was initiated by the president in early 1982 and was headed by J. Peter Grace, chairman of W.R. Grace and Co. Task force reports were completed on the Air Force, Army, Navy, and Office of the Secretary of Defense, as well as on various nondefense activities.

Objects of Reference

Chapter 2 and 4